D0717692
£7.99

CHELSEA'S AMAZING BACK-TO-BACK TITLE TRIUMPH

TRUE BLUE

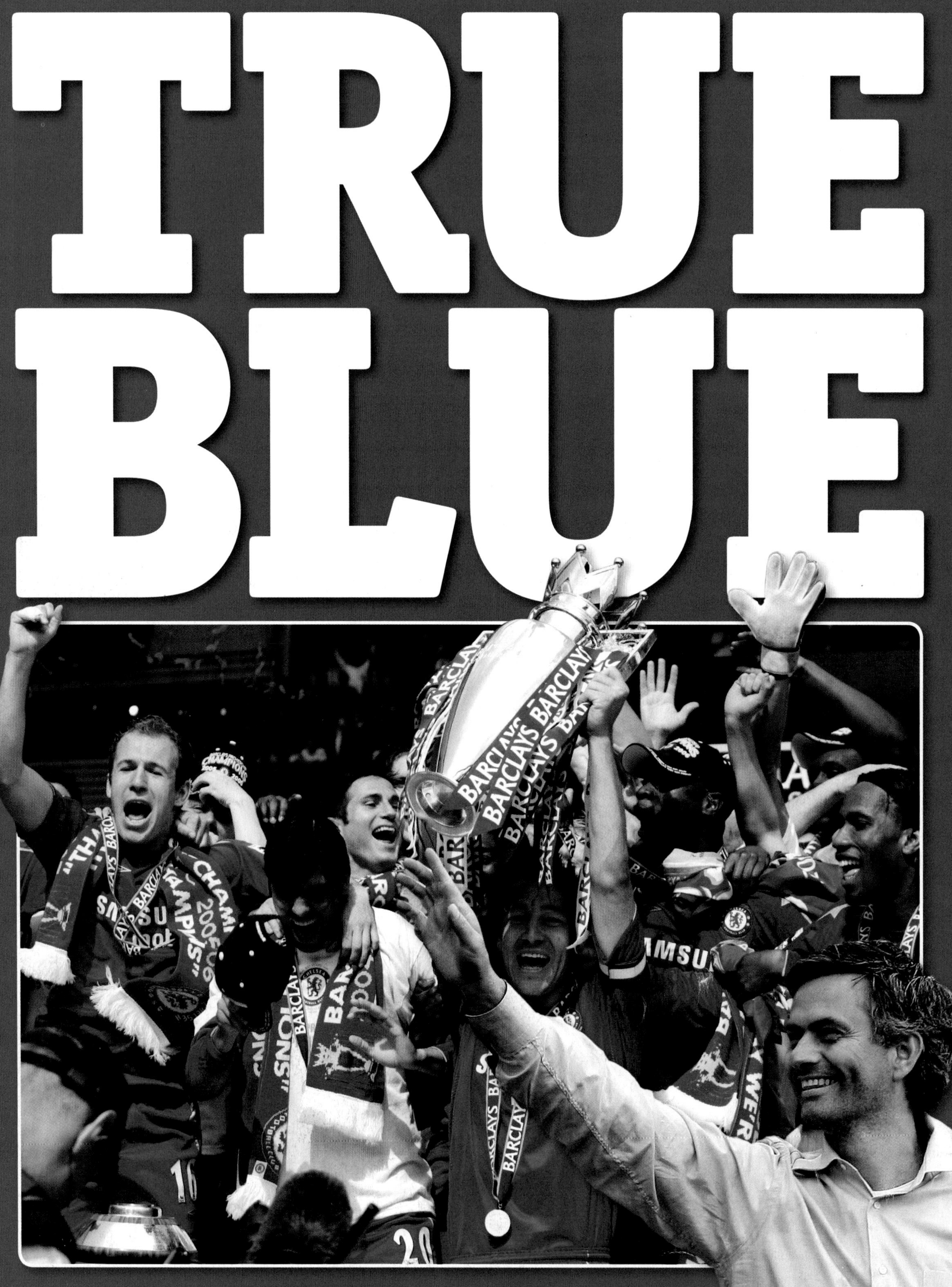

Key men in the title triumph

Petr Cech

Just 24 and already named the No.1 keeper in the world, he kept a total of 21 clean sheets for Chelsea last season.

"So many great goalkeepers, and I was named No.1! It made me proud because my career is only at the beginning. I've learned a lot at Chelsea. Sometimes as a goalkeeper you only reach this stage of your career when you are 30, so I'm some years in advance of that. I just hope I can keep going at this level as long as I can."

John Terry

Skipper John Terry is Chelsea's natural-born leader, the rock at the heart of their defence with a happy knack of scoring goals.

"We're more than just a group of footballers at Chelsea, we're more like brothers. We're in each others' pockets 24 hours a day. The manager has really encouraged us to be a tight unit and believes a strong team spirit will give us an edge over our rivals. When any one of us is feeling down we know the other lads will pick us up.

"We want to win the Premiership for many years to come. We also want to get our hands on the Champions League and the domestic cups. We are committed to remaining the best side in England and have to use our success to take us forward."

Frank Lampard

Frank's 20 goals in all competitions last campaign made him Chelsea's top scorer for a second successive season.

"I wouldn't say I'm like a striker in the way they crave goals, but it gives me a kick being top of the goalscoring chart, seeing my name even above the Van Nistelrooys and Henrys.

"Getting 30 in a calendar year, though, and 20 in a season, became a bit of a target and I'm really pleased with what I've done."

CHELSEA'S CHAMPIONSHIP YEARS

		HOME					AWAY						
2004-05	**P**	**W**	**D**	**L**	**F**	**A**	**W**	**D**	**L**	**F**	**A**	**GD**	**PTS**
1 Chelsea	38	14	5	0	35	6	15	3	1	37	9	57	95
2 Arsenal	38	13	5	1	54	19	12	3	4	33	17	51	83
3 Man United	38	12	6	1	31	12	10	5	4	27	14	32	77
4 Everton	38	12	2	5	24	15	6	5	8	21	31	−1	61

		HOME					AWAY						
2005-06	**P**	**W**	**D**	**L**	**F**	**A**	**W**	**D**	**L**	**F**	**A**	**GD**	**PTS**
1 Chelsea	38	18	1	0	47	9	11	3	5	25	13	50	91
2 Man United	38	13	5	1	37	8	12	3	4	35	26	38	83
3 Liverpool	38	15	3	1	32	8	10	4	5	25	17	32	82
4 Arsenal	38	14	3	2	48	13	6	4	9	20	18	37	67

HOW THE TOP FOUR COMPARED IN THE 2005-06 PREMIERSHIP

- **CLEAN SHEETS:** Liverpool 22, Chelsea 20, Man United 18, Arsenal 16
- **TOP SCORERS:** Thierry Henry (Arsenal) 27, Ruud Van Nistelrooy (Man United) 21, Frank Lampard (Chelsea) 16, Steven Gerrard (Liverpool) 10

The teams and players who collected silverware in 2005-06

READING

CHAMPIONSHIP CHAMPIONS

Skipper Graeme Murty scored a penalty with just six minutes of the final game of the season remaining to give The Royals a 2-1 victory against QPR. His first goal in five years meant every outfield player in the squad had scored and ensured their 106-point total set a new record for the division. They set a new club best of 33 games unbeaten as they left Sheffield United 16 points adrift in the automatic promotion spot. Watford went up after beating Leeds in the play-off final.

SOUTHEND UNITED

LEAGUE ONE CHAMPIONS

Forget Essex girls. The county was the place to be for football with champions Southend and Colchester both getting automatic promotion. It was The Shrimpers second successive promotion following their League Two play-off victory the previous season. Colchester will be playing in the second tier of English football for the first time in their 69-year history. Barnsley beat Swansea in the play-off final.

CARLISLE

LEAGUE TWO CHAMPIONS

Winners of the Conference play-off final in May 2005 after just one season out of League football, Carlisle achieved their second promotion in as many years when they clinched the League Two title exactly a year later. The Cumbrian's Karl Hawley, the division's top scorer with 26 goals, ensured England's most northern club went up. They were joined in automatic promotion by Northampton Town and Leyton Orient. Cheltenham beat Grimsby in the play-off final.

CELTIC

SCOTTISH PREMIER LEAGUE & CIS CUP

The green and white half of Glasgow reclaimed the title and snatched the CIS Cup from Rangers. Hearts separated the two Old Firm sides in the league, a staggering 17 points behind the champions, and one in front of 'Gers. Incredibly, new Parkhead boss Gordon Strachan's first game in charge was a demoralising 5-0 Champions League away defeat to minnows Artmedia. The Bhoys lifted the League Cup with a 3-0 victory over Dunfermline.

ACCRINGTON

CONFERENCE CHAMPIONS

Stanley returned to the League after a 44-year absence. They quit professional football in 1962, folded a year later because of cash problems and began their long fight back in 1968. Hereford beat Halifax in the play-off final.

LIVERPOOL

THE FA CUP

The final FA Cup Final at Cardiff's Millennium Stadium will go down in history as one of the classics of all time. Almost 12m TV viewers in Great Britain saw West Ham take a two-goal lead through a Jamie Carragher own-goal and a Dean Ashton strike. Djibril Cisse pulled one back for The Reds then Steven Gerrard equalised. Paul Konchesky restored The Hammers lead before a stunning 35-yarder from Gerrard, right on time, made it 3-3. Liverpool won the penalty shoot-out 3-1 after extra-time.

MAN UNITED

THE CARLING CUP

Two-goal Wayne Rooney lifted the Man of the Match award as United smashed four past Wigan without reply. Three of the goals came in a match-deciding seven minutes early in the second-half.

HEARTS

SCOTTISH CUP

Premier League Hearts won the trophy but it was Second Division champions Gretna who rightly earned praise. More than 12,000 fans – five times the population of the small borders town – were at Hampden Park to support them. Drawing 1-1 after 90 minutes, they lost 4-1 in the penalty shoot-out.

SWANSEA CITY

FOOTBALL LEAGUE TROPHY

Swansea picked up the trophy for the second time in 12 years thanks to a goal nine minutes from time by striker Adebayo Akinfenwa. Lee Trundle had given The Swans the lead before Adam Murray equalised.

GRAYS ATHLETIC

THE FA TROPHY

Holders Grays beat three-times Trophy winners Woking 2-0 at West Ham's Upton Park thanks to two goals in the last five minutes of the first-half from Dennis Oli and Glenn Poole. Former Woking keeper Ashley Bayes – who saved two penalties in the previous year's final – was Athletic's second-half hero.

NANTWICH TOWN

THE FA VASE

Despite former Chelsea skipper Dennis Wise and Spurs star Dean Austin helping out with training, Hillingdon were beaten 3-1 in the final by Nantwich. Skipper Andy Kinsey grabbed a goal in each half, Stuart Scheuber grabbed a third and sub Leon Nelson got one back.

SEVILLE

UEFA CUP

After amazing comebacks against Basle and Steau Bucharest Middlesbrough's luck finally ran out in Eindhoven when they crashed 4-0 to a slick Seville side. It was Boro's first European final and the last game in charge for Steve McClaren before he took over as England coach.

STEVEN GERRARD

PFA PLAYER OF THE YEAR

The Liverpool skipper rejected Chelsea's attempts to prise him away from his beloved Anfield following the 2005 Champions League victory and showed why he is so valuable to The Reds. Despite being regularly played out of position, the midfielder was the club's top scorer last season with 21 goals.

WAYNE ROONEY

PFA YOUNG PLAYER OF THE YEAR

For the second successive year, England and Manchester United striker Wayne Rooney picked up this award, holding off the challenges of Cristiano Ronaldo, Aaron Lennon, Anton Ferdinand, Darren Bent and Cesc Fabregas. Wayne was also nominated in the senior category.

THE WORLD ACCORDING TO WAYNE ROONEY

ON FAME...

"At home I'm still the same person. Obviously you have to change some of the things you do and grow up a bit faster than a normal teenager would, but I think it is a change for the better. Sometimes it's difficult when you go out somewhere with your girlfriend and there are people watching and taking photographs. But, having said that, I wouldn't swap my job for anything."

ON COLEEN...

"Coleen keeps my feet on the ground. There's no chance of me getting big-headed because she would just say 'behave yourself!' She and all my family make sure I stay as normal and as grounded as I can. It's great to have that fantastic support behind me."

ON HIS DODGY TEMPER...

"I want to enjoy playing and I want to win the game. I'm 110 per cent committed. Sometimes in the past when it hasn't gone right my temperament has let me down a bit. But I'm trying to put that right and I want to do better. Early on in my career I had a lot of bad press about my temperament, but I was only a young lad then. I'm still young, but I've been playing professionally for four years now and I'm learning with every game."

ON HIS SPORTING HERO...

"When I was younger I loved the way Mike Tyson boxed, where he came from. He was more or less adopted. It was a big achievement to be world champion, a great example for any young person."

ON FOOTBALL HEROES...

"You saw the goals Alan Shearer scored for Newcastle. He was probably the best in the league over a ten-year period. Shearer and Paul Gascoigne were probably the two players that I looked up to most when I was younger. Hopefully I can follow them in the way that they played their football which was brilliant."

ON SIR ALEX FERGUSON...

"He is always there watching over training and making sure everything's right. If you have a bad or a good game he'll tell you. But he does like to laugh and joke with the players. He's been really great with me. He is always talking to me before and after games, telling me how he thinks I have played.

"He has been different to what I thought he might be, but he's been brilliant since I signed. He always backs his players through everything and that makes him a great manager. All the players here respect him and I don't think that will ever change."

ON MANCHESTER UNITED...

"'Since I've been at United Sir Alex Ferguson has instilled the winning mentality into me. He does it with every player. He loves to win and if you're not like that then you shouldn't be playing at a club like Man United."

ON WORLD STARS...

"I think Ronaldinho is the best football player in the world. He's a great player. He's strong, quick and he's got good feet and he scores goals and makes goals as well. That's all you can ask from a forward. And then there is Zinedine Zidane. I always loved the way he seemed to glide across the pitch. Brilliant balance, amazing skill and loads of charisma."

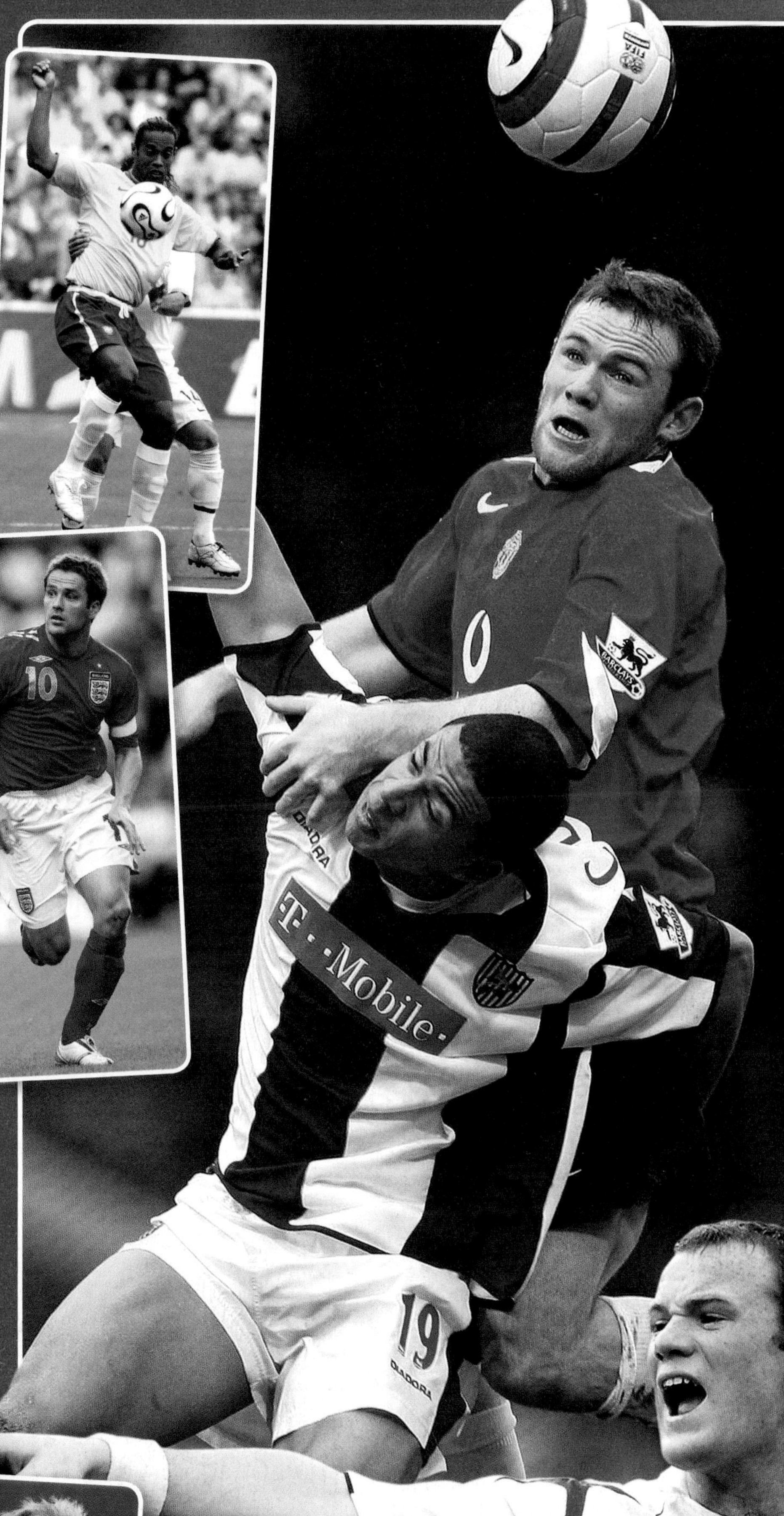

ON MICHAEL OWEN...

"The first World Cup I watched with interest was France 98 really when Michael was a young lad and he did brilliant for England. Obviously he's a fantastic player and he's gone on to score many goals for England and for his clubs as well. Watching that I used to go out and try and be Michael and since then I've been lucky enough to partner him many times for England."

ON HIS LOVE OF FOOTBALL...

"If you ask any of the players, the best thing in training is having a little game and getting loads of chances in a short time, trying to score goals and set them up. And after training I'll go in goal and the lads will take shots. I just love playing football and if I wasn't a professional player and I did a different job, I would be playing Sunday League or at some kind of level."

ON DENNIS BERGKAMP...

"He was a brilliant player who brought others into the game. Look at some of the goals he scored. I think people will look back at Dennis Bergkamp and say that he was one of the best players ever to have played in this country."

THE ONES TO WATCH

We reveal the England youngsters expected to make a BIG name for themselves over the next few years!

BEN ALNWICK, Sunderland

BORN: January 1, 1987, Prudhoe, Northumberland
POSITION: Keeper **Height:** 6ft **Weight:** 12st 9lb

Just 18 when he made his Premiership debut at Arsenal in November 2005, Ben was the star of the team despite being beaten 3-1. He made seven starts for The Black Cats last term, five in the Premier League and two in the League Cup, but a leg injury prevented him adding to that total. Has appeared for England at Under-17, 18 and 19, with four games in the Under-17 European Champs.

GARY CAHILL, Aston Villa

Born: December 19, 1985, Sheffield.
Position: Defender **Height:** 6ft 2in **Weight:** 11st 2lb

A loan to Burnley in 2004-05, where he turned out 32 times and won a number of Man of the Match awards, resulted in Gary returning to Villa. His six Premiership starts and one League Cup appearance last term were enough to earn a lucrative three-year deal at Villa Park.

MICAH RICHARDS, Man City

Born: June 24, 1988, Birmingham
Position: Defender **Height:** 5ft 11in **Weight:** 13st

Arguably one of the finds of last season. He made his debut in October 2005, but once he got back into the side the following February he became a fixture. A confident, tough tackler with the ability to break forward, the big clubs have already had their scouts watching him.

NATHAN ASHTON, Charlton Athletic

Born: January 30, 1987, Plaistow, East London **Position:** Left-back
Height: 5ft 9in **Weight:** 11st 8lb

A regular in The Addicks' reserves and with England Under-20s, ankle injuries have hit his chances of making the first-team at The Valley. But while other prospects from their youth system have left, Nathan has won new contracts and is expected to make the breakthrough soon. He's very fast and has been likened to England regular Ashley Cole.

BILLY JONES, Crewe Alexandra

Born: March 24, 1987, Shrewsbury, Shropshire
Position: Defender **Height:** 5ft 11in **Weight:** 13st

Six Championship goals and one in the FA Cup made him Crewe's top scorer last term. Not bad for a defender who made his Crewe debut at 15. Billy has captained England Under-18s, as well as playing for the Under-19s, and has been likened to former England and Arsenal skipper Tony Adams, his personal hero.

LEE CATTERMOLE, Middlesbrough

Born: March 21, 1988, Stockton-on-Tees
Position: Midfield **Height:** 5ft 10in **Weight:** 12st

Local lad Lee made his debut last January in the Tyne-Tees derby against Newcastle and went on to make an impressive 17 appearances before the end of the season. Hard as nails, he can also pass the ball and didn't look out of place in the Premiership, or against tough opposition as Boro reached the final of the UEFA Cup. He came on in place of Mark Viduka in the final, but the game had already been lost. A product of The Riverside's youth academy, he has already appeared for England Under-16s, 17s and 18s.

CAMERON JEROME, Birmingham

Born: August 14, 1986, Huddersfield
Position: Striker **Height:** 6ft 1in **Weight:** 13st 6lb

Released as a youth by Huddersfield, and allowed to leave Middlesbrough without playing a first-team game, Cameron hit the goals jackpot at Cardiff City, finishing last term as their top scorer with 20. That earned the England Under-21 marksman a move to Birmingham City for an initial £3m fee which could rise to £4m if he can help The Blues win promotion back to the Premiership.

MARK NOBLE, West Ham

Born: May 8, 1987, Canning Town, East London **Position:** Midfield
Height: 5ft 11in **Weight:** 12st 3lb

With the club since he was 12, Mark gate-crashed the promotion-winning side of 2005, and made 15 appearances, including coming on as a sub in the play-off games. He was loaned out to Hull at the end of last term to gain more experience, but The Hammers have the former England Under-18 captain under contract until 2009.

DANIEL STURRIDGE, Man City

Born: September 9, 1989
Position: Striker **Height:** 5ft 11in **Weight:** 12st

Chelsea, Barcelona and Arsenal have already checked out Danny, nephew of former pros Dean and Simon. And the experts reckon he could be sold for in excess of the £12m paid by The Gunners for Theo Walcott. He's a natural finisher with a load of goals already to his name at all England levels up to Under-17s.

PETER RAMAGE, Newcastle

Born: November 22, 1983, Whitley Bay **Position:** Defender **Height:** 6ft 1in **Weight:** 11st 3lb

Peter had made just four appearances before last season but, having been called up to cover for injuries, he became a first-team fixture. Regarded as a central-defender, he played in every position across the back line. A no-nonsene product of the club's academy.

JOE GARNER, Blackburn

Born: April 12, 1988, Blackburn **Position:** Striker **Height:** 5ft 10in **Weight:** 10st 12lb

The name Garner is already etched in Rovers' history thanks to Simon, their record goal-scorer. Joe has a big task to follow that act, but he's already proved a prolific hit-man at academy and reserve level for Blackburn. He also scored eight goals in just 14 games at England Under-17 level and has even made the step up to Under-19s.

RYAN SMITH, Arsenal

Born: November 10, 1986, Islington, North London **Position:** Winger **Height:** 5ft 10in **Weight:** 10st 7lb

Left-footed, quick, an eye for goal and a great crosser – no wonder Arsene Wenger predicts a bright future for Ryan. After the youngster bounced back from a cruciate injury, his boss loaned him to Leicester last season where he made a big impression, playing 19 games. He was asked to stay, but his future appears at Ashburton Grove.

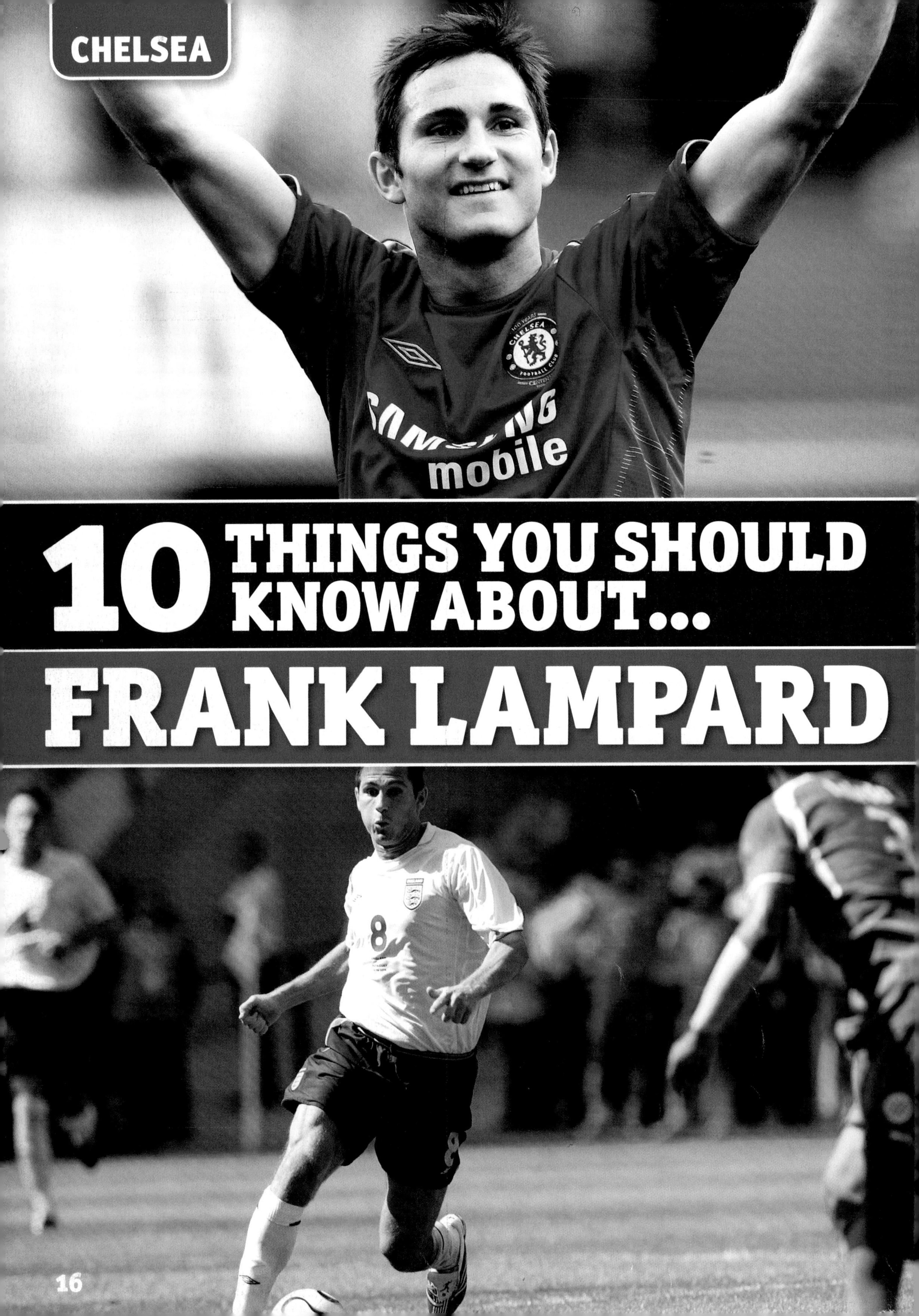

10 THINGS YOU SHOULD KNOW ABOUT...

FRANK LAMPARD

1 Frank was born on June 20, 1978 in Romford, Essex. His dad, (Frank senior) is a former England full-back and also won the FA Cup twice with West Ham.

2 Frank's uncle is Portsmouth manager Harry Redknapp and his cousin is ex-England star Jamie Redknapp.

3 He joined West Ham United, where his dad was assistant manager, as an apprentice in July 1994. He later had a spell out on loan at Swansea City before becoming a regular Hammer over the next seven years.

4 Fed up that his close mate Rio Ferdinand was sold to Leeds United in the 2000-01 season, and that his father and uncle left West Ham, Frank decided to leave as well. Chelsea paid a whopping £11m for his services in May 2001.

5 He has been sent off only once in his career – in his fourth Premiership game for Chelsea, against Spurs on September 16, 2001. His 16 goals in the 2005-2006 season is a record for a midfielder in the Premier League.

6 Frank's other half, Elen Rives, is Spanish and Frank can talk the lingo like a natural. That has led many to believe that he may move to La Liga one day. He himself has said: "Barcelona are my favourite team in Spain, let's put it that way."

7 He is the only member of the England team to have gone to a private school, having attended the £10,000-a-year Brentwood School in Essex. And guess what? He was in the same year as model Jodie Marsh!

8 In 2005 he was voted runner-up to Ronaldinho, both in the European Footballer of the Year award and the FIFA World Player of the Year Award.

9 Frank is a huge cricket nut. He said he went "ballistic" when England won the Ashes on home soil.

10 Frank played every minute of every England game in the World Cup – and had more shots than anyone else!

IT'S A FUNNY OLD GAME!

A LOOK AT THE CRAZY WORLD OF FOOTBALL

Spiderman's goal wasn't enough as a second half Batman hat trick won the game. Okay, we're lying – it's Ecuador's Ivan Kaviedes scoring against Costa Rica.

Ruud Van Nistelrooy has a strange way of taking the dog for a walk.

Ronaldo needed a little bit of help getting his contact lenses in.

Bolton's Vaz Te and Faye failed their audition for Strictly Come Dancing.

To prove there's no hard feelings Wayne, I'll buy you a KFC tonight.

Although diving became popular at the World Cup, this fan took it too far.

Claude Makelele wished a can of RightGuard came with the winners medal.

The Cardboard One takes his place on the Chelsea bench.

Graham Poll, decides to drown his sorrows after a disastrous World Cup.

KNOW YOUR FOOTBALL?

Find out if you are a footie brainbox with our great quiz!

WHO SCORED?

DATE: June 25, 2006 **VENUE:** Stuttgart
MATCH: England v Ecuador **RESULT:** 1-0
Name the goal scorer from the players below:

A – Steven Gerrard B – John Terry
C – Frank Lampard D – David Beckham

TRIVIAL TEAZERS

1. In which city was last season's Champions League Final played?

2. Which Championship club play at Elland Road?

3. Which South American team did England play in the group stage of last summer's World Cup in Germany?

4. From which club did Everton sign striker Andy Johnson?

5. Name the Premiership manager who used to play for Charlton and Crystal Palace.

6. What colours do you traditionally associate with Norwich City?

7. Who scored more goals for England; Robbie Fowler or Teddy Sheringham?

8. Howard Webb, Steve Bennett and Rob Styles are all what?

9. Who scored Liverpool's first goal in last season's FA Cup Final v West Ham?

10. Which club are nicknamed "The Blades"?

WHICH SPORTING VENUE?

Which is the nearest Premiership club to each of these sporting events?

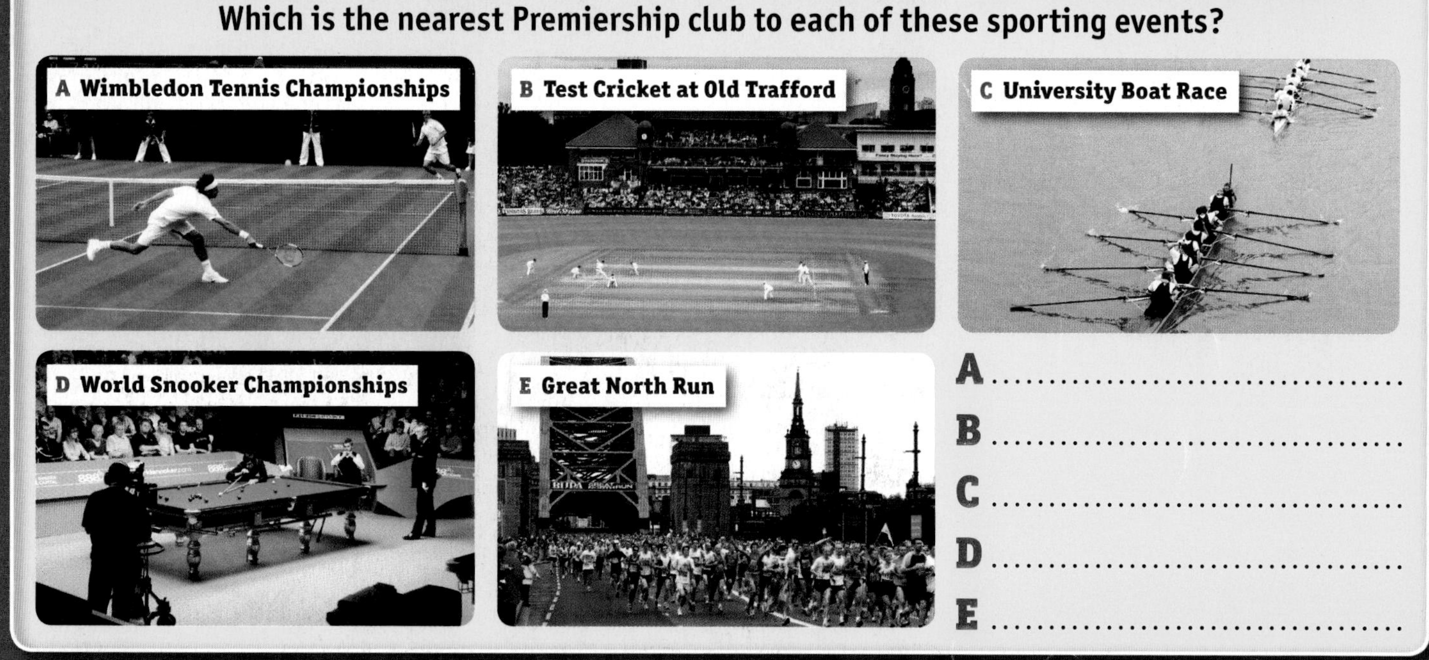

A ....
B ....
C ....
D ....
E ....

NAME THE HIDDEN FACES

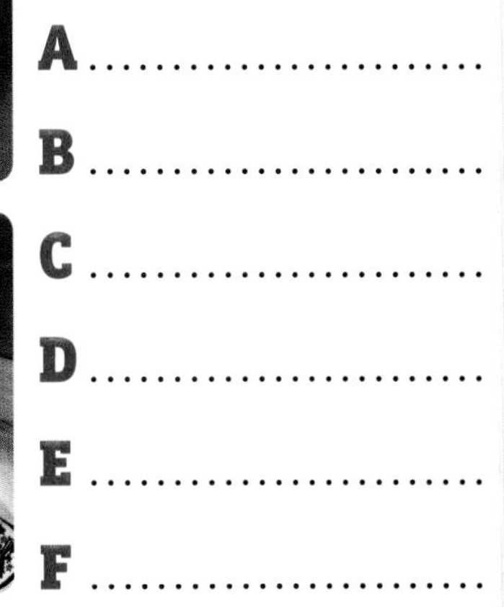

Name the following football people below:

A ....

B ....

C ....

D ....

E ....

F ....

GOALMOUTH SCRAMBLE

Unscramble the letters below to find the names of ten former Champions League winners.

1. MACNAIL
2. TROOP
3. USTEVENUJ
4. REALSLIME
5. ACREBLOAN
6. MRSTENCHDETAINUE
7. DRMEALRAID
8. BARUNCHIMNEY
9. DDRUSSIABROOMNUT
10. OLIVERLOP

SPOTTHEBALL

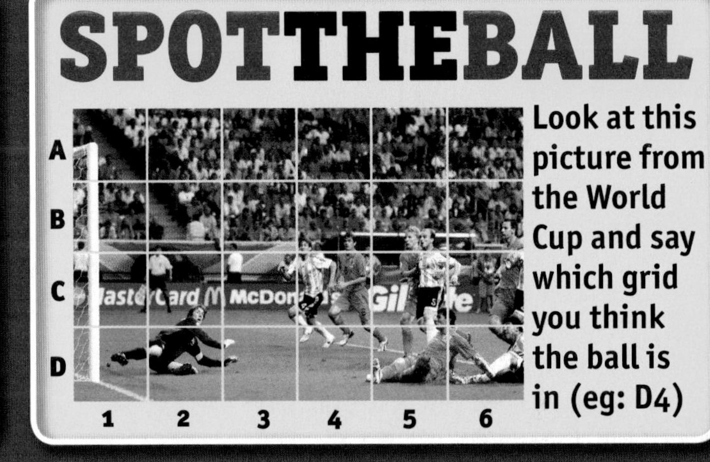

Look at this picture from the World Cup and say which grid you think the ball is in (eg: D4)

MISSINGLINKS

Robbie Savage

Fill in the missing links below to identify which players have played for which clubs:

1. **Robbie Keane:** Wolves, Coventry, Inter Milan, ..., Tottenham.
2. ....: Liverpool, Leeds, Manchester City, Liverpool.
3. **Robbie Savage:** Crewe, ..., Birmingham, Blackburn.
4. ....: Watford, Liverpool, Aston Villa, West Ham, Manchester City.
5. **Lee Bowyer:** Charlton, Leeds, ..., Newcastle, West Ham.

NAME THAT YEAR

Name the year in which all of the following happened:

1. Celtic lost to Porto in the UEFA Cup Final.
2. West Ham were relegated from the Premiership.
3. Robert Pires scored the winning goal in the FA Cup Final.

Answers on pages 110

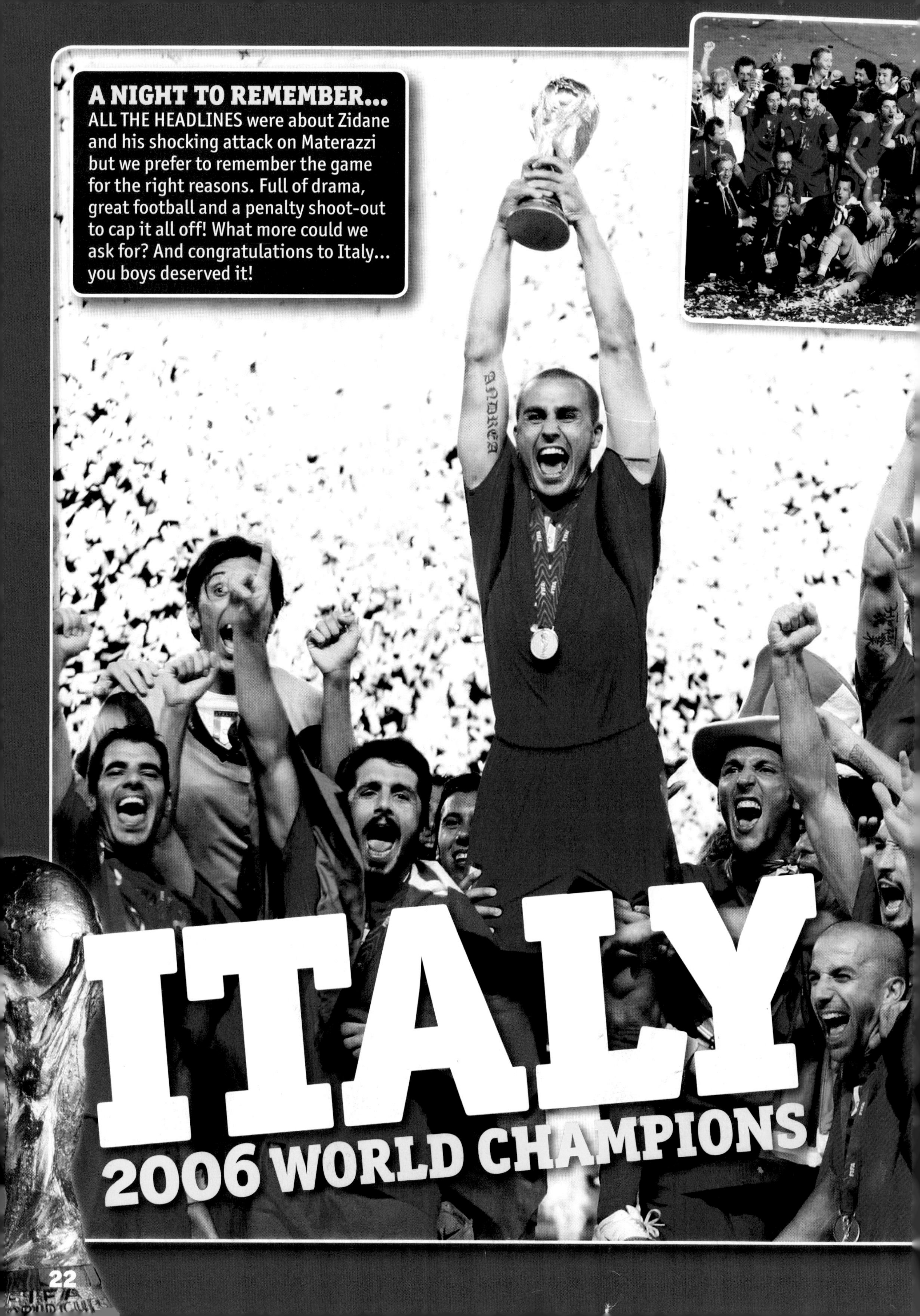

A NIGHT TO REMEMBER...

ALL THE HEADLINES were about Zidane and his shocking attack on Materazzi but we prefer to remember the game for the right reasons. Full of drama, great football and a penalty shoot-out to cap it all off! What more could we ask for? And congratulations to Italy... you boys deserved it!

ITALY

2006 WORLD CHAMPIONS

SHOOT AWARDS

BEST GOAL: Esteban Cambiasso (Argentina)
The 24-pass stunner against Serbia and Montenegro (right).

BEST PLAYER: Fabio Cannavaro (Italy)
No-nonsense defender and inspirational captain.

BEST COACH: Marcello Lippi (Italy)
For leading his team to World Cup glory when the national game was in turmoil.

MOST ANIMATED COACH: Luiz Felipe Scolari (Portugal)
Was "Big Phil" (right) getting over-involved or did he just have ants in his pants?

LEAST ANIMATED: Sven Goran Eriksson (England)
Stuck to the bench – did he have superglue on his bum?!

SHOCK RESULT: Ghana beating the Czech Republic
The result was 2-0 but if it wasn't for goalie Petr Cech, it could have been a lot more.

WORST BARNET: Mauro Camoranesi (Italy)
The Italian midfielder (left) had a shocker.

BEST SULKER: Oliver Kahn (Germany)
We think Oliver (right) may have been a little bit upset about being Germany's second choice keeper. What do you think?

TOURNAMENT BOO-BOY: Cristiano Ronaldo (Portugal)
We love Ronaldo (left) for his football. Not so sure about all that diving nonsense!

DRAMATIC MOMENT: Zinedine Zidane loses plot
French captain headbutted Materazzi in the Final. What a rotten way to end a great career...

EMBARRASSING MOMENT: Graham Poll loses the plot
English ref thinks it would be funky to give Croatia's Simunic THREE yellows.

BEST LOOKING FANS: Brazilians
Look at this picture – nuff said...

FULL NAME:
Luiz Nazario de Lima

DATE OF BIRTH:
September 21, 1976

PLACE OF BIRTH:
Bento Ribeiro,
Rio de Janeiro, Brazil

NICKNAMES:
"The Phenomenon",
"Boy Wonder",
"The Kid"

RONALDO WE SALUTE YOU!

A tribute to record-breaking Brazilian legend Ronaldo...

ALTHOUGH THE WORLD CUP was a disappointing tournament for Brazil overall, at least one man has an excuse for showing off his trademark grin.

Ronaldo, Brazil's top striker for nearly a decade, reached an impressive World Cup landmark in 2006, breaking the record for goals scored in the tournament. But this is only the latest in a long line of triumphs for the legendary hitman. Here **Shoot** gets its teeth (sorry Ronny) into his amazing World Cup career thus far...

Ronaldo's Roll of Honour

- Brazilian Cup Cruzeiro 1993
- Dutch Cup PSV Eindhoven 1996
- Spanish Super Cup Barcelona 1996
- Cup Winners' Cup Barcelona 1997
- Confederations Cup 1997
- Copa America 1997
- FIFA World Player of the Year 1996, 1997
- European Footballer of the Year 1997
- UEFA Champions League Most Valuable Player 1997-1998
- FIFA World Cup Golden Ball 1998
- UEFA Cup Inter Milan 1998
- Copa America 1999
- European Footballer of the Year 2002
- FIFA World Player of the Year 2002
- FIFA World Cup Golden Shoe 2002
- European Super Cup Real Madrid 2002
- Intercontinental Cup Real Madrid 2002
- La Liga Real Madrid 2002-2003
- Most goals(15) in FIFA WC History 2006
- Spanish Super Cup Real Madrid 2003

1 Ronaldo first appeared for Brazil in a friendly against Argentina (March 1994) but the 17-year-old did not feature in USA 94 despite making the squad (right).

2 Ronaldo won the FIFA World Player of the Year awards in 1996 and 1997 and went into France 98 full of confidence. He scored four goals on the way to the Final but was taken ill before the showpiece event. Despite this convulsive fit, he took to the field but looked a shadow of his former self (left). France emerged 3-0 winners

3 The next four years were largely ruined by injury, a long-standing knee complaint saw his build-up to Japan/Korea 2002 ruined. Yet, even though struggling for form and fitness, Brazil coach Luiz Felipe Scolari included him in the squad – and what a decision it proved! Ronaldo became the tournament's top scorer, netting eight goals in seven games (above) and helping The Samba Boys lift the trophy.

4 A familiar story as Ronaldo again faced a race against time to be fit for Germany 06. After a slow start, his third goal of the tournament and his 15th in all World Cups, against Ghana (below) broke the finals scoring record, previously held by West Germany's Gerd Muller. He also became the only player, other than Jurgen Klinsmann, to score three goals in three World Cups.

He said: "For me this World Cup won't be my last. Four years from now, I hope to be physically healthy and motivated to play one more."

ENGLAND

PAY THE PENALTY – AGAIN!

ENGLAND players thought they could win the World Cup. They thought wrong. The Three Lions whimpered to the quarter-finals where they once again fell victim to the dreaded penalty shoot-out, crashing out of the competition to Portugal. The route to their final game at Germany 06 wasn't very smooth either...!

GROUP STAGE

PARAGUAY 1-0

An own-goal after three minutes – a Beckham free-kick being deflected into the net – gave England a dream start but in the blistering heat they failed to push on. Still, they normally start tournaments slowly, so three points was a satisfactory opener.

TRINIDAD & TOBAGO 2-0

Early promise turned to fans' groans as passes went astray and it was seven minutes before the end before Peter Crouch headed a Beckham cross after a series of misses. Steven Gerrard's trademark screamer right on time gave the result respectability

GROUP STAGE

GROUP STAGE

SWEDEN 2-2

Joe Cole scored one of the goals of the tournament with a 35-yard lob after 34 minutes, but six minutes after the break Sweden were level with Marcus Allback's header, the 2,000th goal in the history of the finals. Five minutes from time Gerrard headed in a Cole cross, but they failed to hang on as Henrik Larsson equalised right on time. England have failed to beat the Swedes since 1968.

ECUADOR 1-0

SECOND ROUND

Becks' free-kick, which sailed into the top corner to give England victory, was the only highlight. The goal made him the first England player to score at three World Cups. It was his first international goal in 13 games and his first direct from a free-kick for three years.

QUARTER-FINAL

PORTUGAL 0-0 (PORTUGAL WON 3-1 ON PENS)

England were totally unconvincing – and only started to show their fighting spirit after Wayne Rooney was sent off on the hour for allegedly stamping on Chelsea's Carvalho. They hung on for the last 30 minutes and bravely battled through extra-time only to fall victim once again to a penalty shoot-out. Only Owen Hargreaves scored as Frank Lampard, Steven Gerrard and Jamie Carragher all failed from the spot. England were out and Becks resigned the captaincy soon after.

"Wayne is one of the best strikers in the world and you're cutting one of his legs off if you play one up front. Player for player, I'm still convinced we were the best team in the tournament, yet we were out in the quarter-finals again." **Striker Michael Owen.**

"We have come in for criticism in the past for not practising penalties but I can assure you, we had been practising them all the time after going to Germany. When it goes to penalties it is a lottery and we came unstuck again. Every one of us felt we could go all the way this time and it is such a shame it ended like it did." **Liverpool hit-man Peter Crouch.**

"When the referee produced the red card I was amazed – gobsmacked. What happened didn't warrant a red card. If anything, I feel we should have had a free-kick for the fouls committed on me during the same incident." **Wayne Rooney on his sending-off against Portugal.**

"There were a lot of the lads in the dressing room really upset. This is a proud footballing nation. We lost, we suffer, but we pick ourselves up. It is the English mentality – you fight back, you don't give anything away." **Gary Neville, who missed vital games.**

A-Z OF THE WORLD CUP

From Argentina to Zidane, our whistle-stop tour of the World Cup

A Argentina

After they blew Serbia and Montenegro away 6-0 AND scored that 24-pass goal of the tournament, everyone thought they'd go on to lift the World Cup. But they didn't count on those pesky Germans who NEVER lose penalty shoot-outs!

B Bye Bye Becks

David Beckham stood down as captain after England's exit to Portugal. Thanks for the memories Becks, we'll miss ya...

C Cry Babies

What was it about this World Cup? We expect from that big girl's blouse Cristiano Ronaldo and maybe the super-sensitive David Beckham. But never thought we'd see the big fella John Terry turning on the waterworks too!

D Diving

It was a great World Cup with loads of exciting football to keep us on the edge of our seats. But there was way too much diving. Even Thierry Henry – who we think is a legend – got in on the act against Spain. And don't even get us started on Portugal...

E Embrace

No we're not talking about England players getting all cuddly. Instead, we're on about England's official tournament anthem, "World at Your Feet" recorded by Embrace. It didn't mention the word "football" anywhere in the lyrics, so to be fair we won't mention the words "rubbish song". Whoops, just did.

F Free-kick

Okay England didn't play well. But wasn't Becks' free-kick against Ecuador a corker?

G Germany

Written off before the World Cup had begun, the host nation managed to get to the semis playing some smashing football. In fact they scored 14 goals, the highest amount by any team in the tournament.

H Hargreaves

While all around him lost their heads, Owen emerged as England's player of the tournament.

Whether at right-back or in a holding midfield role, the Bayern star proved to everyone that he can cut the mustard at this level.

I Italy

No prizes for guessing what we'd pick here. The World Champions – brilliantly led by Fabio Cannavaro –deservedly won the trophy because they peaked at the right time. Their achievement is remarkable seeing as Italian football was in crisis.

J Jurgen

What a manager! Some older readers may remember Jurgen from his playing spell at Spurs a few years back but he's now a wicked coach! Germany will miss him now he's resigned...

K Kick

We're talking about Wayne Rooney's "stamp" on Portugal's Ricardo Carvalho in the quarter-final. We'll leave it up to you to decide whether it was deliberate or not. Either way, with the Roonster's red card, so too went England's World Cup hopes.

L Lippi

Italian coach Marcello Lippi masterminded Italy's World Cup triumph. Not bad for an old fella eh?

M Maradona

One of the lingering memories from the World Cup was the wee fella going berserk in the stands every time Argentina scored. But what's going on with that barnet?

N Nuremberg

More than 70,000 England fans (a lot of them without tickets) descended on this German town for the Trinidad and Tobago game, and there was virtually no bother. Shows that not all our supporters are trouble-makers!

O Organisation

Shoot was lucky enough to go to the World Cup (yes, we're bragging). Thanks to our German hosts for putting on a really well-organised and friendly tournament.

P Penalty Shoot-out

When are England ever gonna win one of these? As soon as the quarter-final against Portugal went to penalties, we all knew the result. This time Frank Lampard, Steven Gerrard and Jamie Carragher were the fall-guys.

Q Quickest

The quickest goal of the World Cup was scored by Ghana's Asamoah Gyan against the Czech Republic. He hit the back of the net after just one minute and eight seconds!

R Ronaldo

We're talking about the Brazilian one, not the Portuguese git! Yes he was a bit porky but his strike against Ghana in the second round still took him to 15 World Cup goals – that's a record.

S Sven

When he first took over the England job, Sven said that 2006 was going to be our year. Yeah right! He's trousered £25m in five years as England coach – at least someone's happy!

T Trezeguet

Someone always has to miss in a penalty shoot-out but poor David Trezeguet's shot against the bar in the final crushed French hopes.

U — Underdog

Our shock of the World Cup award goes to Ghana's brilliant 2-0 win over the Czech Republic. If goalkeeper Petr Cech hadn't been on form, it could've been 7-0!

V — Villain

Who else but Cristiano Ronaldo? Not only did he dive all over the place but helped get Wayne Rooney sent off too. And we all saw that cheeky wink...

W — WAGS

The England team's "Wives And Girlfriends" almost made more headlines in Germany than the football. Their non-stop partying and shopping was great for the local businesses but probably not so good for the players' bank balances...

X — X-Ray

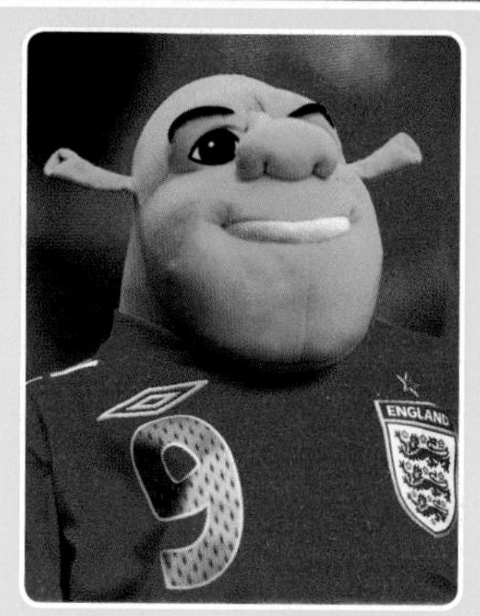

Oooh the irony. We spend most of the build-up panicking about Wayne Rooney's x-rays and whether he will be fit or not, only for Shrek junior to go and blow it all against Portugal. Wonder if they x-rayed his head, whether they'd find a brain... only joking Wayne!

Y — Yellow Cards

Three of 'em! All issued to Croatia's Josip Simunic by English referee Graham Poll. Now listen carefully Graham – two yellows equals a red. Got that?

Z — Zidane

Oh Zizou. What were you thinking? The most exciting player of his generation had an opportunity to mark his retirement with another World Cup win, only to literally see red in the final. He let himself down and his country – even if that Materazzi bloke looks like he needed a good slap!

Germany knocked Argentina out in the quarter-finals and then the Argies tried to knock-out the Germans – literally.

Wayne Rooney "kicks-off" after being taken off against Sweden.

Sssssh, don't tell anyone I'm fouling you. Zinedine Zidane is held back by Switzerland's Johann Vogel.

Arsenal's Philippe Senderos headed both ball and man as he scored Switzerland's first goal against South Korea.

ARGY!

Some of the thrills and spills from this year's World Cup extravaganza.

Fulham striker Brian McBride was on the receiving end of a flying Italian elbow belonging to Danielle De Rossi.

Ricardo Carvalho feels the force of Wayne Rooney's healed metatarsal.

A Zizou header shocked Marco Materazzi and the whole world in the Final.

Portugal and Holland shared 16 yellow and four red cards in this battle.

Italy coach Marcello Lippi shows his frustration during the final.

GAME ON!

England players don't like losing. And we don't just mean at football. Away from the World Cup action on the pitch, they were battling it out to see who was best at table-tennis, golf, darts, cards, board games and computer games...

COMPUTER GAMES

Ashley Cole is the king at arcade-style games. But he has a tough rival at ISS on PS2. "I think Jermaine Jenas is the man," said Jermain Defoe.

"Michael Carrick is good, he plays all the time, and I know Rio Ferdinand practises! He says he isn't bothered, but he is.

"The Chelsea boys are good too: Joe Cole and John Terry - Ashley Cole and Wayne Rooney as well.

"After training we get back to the rooms and play a little tournament after dinner."

TABLE-TENNIS

Jermain Defoe missed out on the World Cup, otherwise he would have been a contender on the table-tennis table.

His agent, Sky Andrew, is a former British table-tennis champion, so there's plenty of opportunity for a bit of sneaky coaching!

But when it comes to ping-pong, look no further than Rio Ferdinand!

"I'm the best table-tennis player in football, no doubt about that," said the Man United defender. "If there is anyone out there capable of beating me, bring it on."

CARDS

Manager Sven Goran Eriksson allowed his stars to play cards at the finals – poker and three-card brag were the most popular games – but restricted the bets.

Players were encouraged to play for points – with no more than a £200-a-person kitty up for grabs for the overall winner.

BOARD GAMES

Trivial Pursuit and Monopoly were ordered for England's hotel drawing room and even that proved competitive. There was also a Scrabble board, a favourite with brainbox keeper David James, a man never lost for words.

DARTS

Chelsea skipper John Terry is king of the oche – but only if you believe his own hype!

"I look forward to the darts," he said. "We've got a dart board at the Chelsea training ground and I'm not bad! All the lads practise after we come off the pitch."

HE IS THE ONE AND OWENLY!

There's one man they all fear when it comes to games off the pitch, all-rounder Michael Owen.

The Newcastle striker is an ace on the snooker table, as well as being one of the best golfers in the England squad. He's also particularly good at cards, owns a racehorse and is a pretty mean cricketer.

"I think I'm lucky because when I was a lad I didn't just play football," said Michael. "My dad had me trying everything. I played golf, cricket, snooker, played in two or three football teams at a time, did athletics with the county, rugby, even a bit of boxing for three and a half years. So I've had a grounding in lots of sports."

MODEL PROS

Don't let 'em fool you. They spend most of their lives in the public eye and they secretly love it!

Ronaldinho The Brazilian superstar dances to the Samba drum on the pitch and can play a mean tune off it.

James Beattie With Andy Johnson joining the striking ranks at Everton, James won't want to be left on the bench.

Patrick Vieira When he retires from football the former Arsenal star looks like he has a new snooker career lined up.

Joe Cole One of few shining lights at a disappointing World Cup for England, Joe looks Mr Cool on and off the pitch.

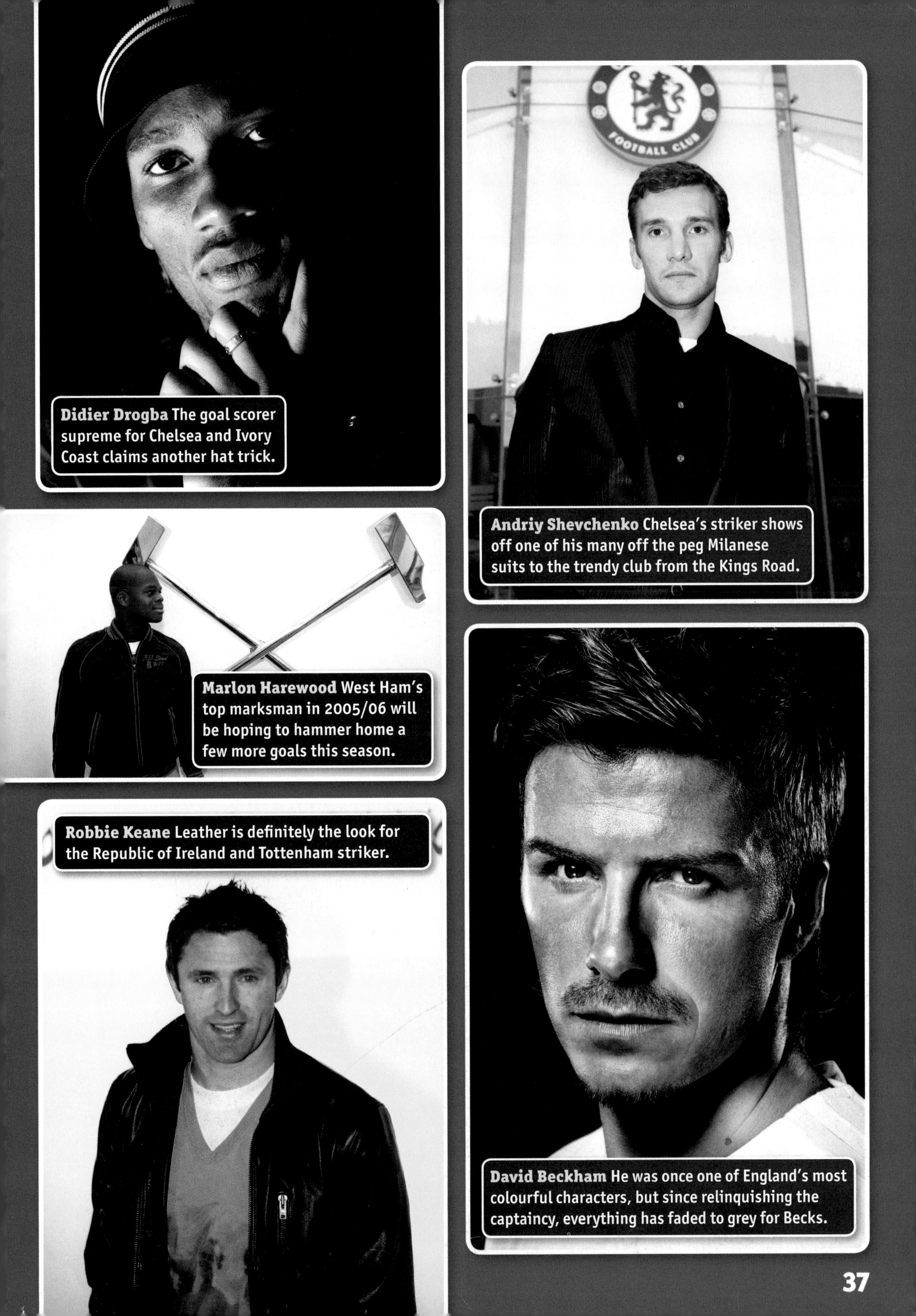

Didier Drogba The goal scorer supreme for Chelsea and Ivory Coast claims another hat trick.

Andriy Shevchenko Chelsea's striker shows off one of his many off the peg Milanese suits to the trendy club from the Kings Road.

Marlon Harewood West Ham's top marksman in 2005/06 will be hoping to hammer home a few more goals this season.

Robbie Keane Leather is definitely the look for the Republic of Ireland and Tottenham striker.

David Beckham He was once one of England's most colourful characters, but since relinquishing the captaincy, everything has faded to grey for Becks.

PUTTIN' ON A SHOW!

Behind the scenes with Sky Sports at the 2006 Champions League Final between Arsenal and Barcelona...

When Arsenal headed to Paris to take on Barcelona last May, it took the number of Champions League games covered live by Sky Sports last season to 103.

For their regular Monday night live games Sky use up to 25 cameras, eight trucks and five miles of cable. For this final, however, the French TV network TF1 acted as host broadcaster.

But Sky Sports programme director Mike Allen said: "The host director has to work within certain criteria laid down by UEFA to keep the coverage consistent so we have a good idea about what we're getting.

"We just wrap the present nicely by topping and tailing the pictures from TF1 with our own graphics, replays, studio coverage and the like. That alone required us taking 85 crew to Paris, along with two of our own outside broadcast trucks. But a lot of the work is about making sure that all the hardware plugs in and works."

Sky Sports commentator and **Shoot** columnist, Martin Tyler, who was covering the game, admitted: "To me, all the games on which I commentate are exciting. The last thing I would want is to sound different just because I am covering the Champions League Final.

"I watched Barcelona training at the stadium the day before and managed to name all 22 of the players involved, which I was quite pleased about. It's not the big names but the squad players and the unexpected substitutions which can be the pitfalls for commentators.

"I told Andy Gray that I was going to watch Barca on Sky Sports the previous weekend. He said it wouldn't be worth it as none of the big names would be involved. But that was exactly why I wanted to watch it!"

TIMELINE

MONDAY

- **8am** Trucks park up at underground facility in stadium
- **10am** Technical rigging begins
- **12pm** Broadcast computing and graphics on site
- **5pm** Vision check takes place to ensure all is in order

TUESDAY

- **11am** Shoots around Paris, stadium and press conferences
- **2pm** Production meeting
- **3.30pm** Rehearsal
- **7.30pm** Preview show live - the best build-up to the final. When Sky do it, they don't do it by halves!

Sky Sports' programme director Mike Allen orchestrates proceedings from inside one of the OB trucks.

Sky's two state-of-the-art OB trucks park up under the stadium. With broadcasters from all over Europe doing the same, the bowels of the Stade de France resemble a makeshift TV town.

Key camera positions behind the goal. The game is filmed by French network TF1, from which Sky take a feed. But many TV stations will also have a small number of camera positions of their own.

WEDNESDAY

- **1pm** Production crew on site
- **2pm** Production crew check facilities
- **2.30pm** Rehearsal
- **3.30pm** Electronic circuits up and running
- **4.30pm** Meal break
- **5.50pm** Rehearsal
- **7pm** On-air
- **11.30pm** Off-air

Something tickles Sky Sports' presenter Richard Keys as he reads through his script during the afternoon's rehearsal...

Not as big as it seems! Inside the tight confines of Sky's temporary studio at the stadium.

Up on the roof! Reporter Jim White, broadcasting live, reports from a roof-top opposite the stadium.

Pushing the buttons – members of the crew operating the highly sophisticated hardware inside an OB truck.

TV Town beneath the Stade de France.

Each of the networks gets a small room somewhere deep in the stadium to use as a makeshift HQ.

The Mixed Zone – the area set up for pre and post-match player interviews, complete with sponsor backdrops.

Sky pundits Ruud Gullit and Jamie Redknapp contemplate a kick-about.

Togged up and ready for action – Richard Keys views the pitch from the temporary studio.

"Hey Jamie, did you know that Milan only signed Ruud coz they couldn't get me...???" Paul Merson, Sky Sports panellist No.3.

"Yer doing it all wrong son...!" Jamie, under the watchful eye of Mr Merson.

Cable, cable and more cable....

Reporter Nick Collins chats with a colleague: "Yesterday's pre-match press conference had more TV crews than I've ever seen at such an event. You had to get there two hours early to get near!"

"I could have been a contender you know Jamie..." Richard Keys shows the pros how it's done.

Arch-rivals! Sky's Martin Tyler compares notes with ITV's Andy Townsend.

"Tel, we're havin' a kick-about – come and be manager!"

"Hey Merse – heard about this kick-about? Fancy re-creating some of the old Arsenal magic?"

"Fancy it Coisty? Come on, we'll do Ruud easily, won't we gaffer?"

"I'd just like to say on record that I'm not getting involved in this ridiculous kick-about with Jamie Redknapp."

10 THINGS YOU SHOULD KNOW ABOUT...

RONALDINHO

1 Born on March 21, 1980, in Porto Alegre, Brazil, his real name is Ronaldo de Assis Moreira. Ronaldinho is Portuguese for "little Ronaldo" and was a way of distinguishing himself from the "other" Ronaldo!

2 He started his career at Brazilian club Gremio (Big Phil Scolari was coach), then he went to Paris St. Germain before joining Barcelona - for whom he turned down Manchester United. Hard luck Fergie!

3 He once scored 23 goals in a single game as a 13-year-old in local youth football at home in Brazil.

4 Ronaldinho has been awarded the FIFA World Player of the Year award twice, as well as both the European Footballer of the Year award and the FIFPro World Player of the Year award.

5 His father João was a shipyard worker and amateur footballer. Tragically, he died when Ronaldinho was eight after suffering a heart attack in the family's swimming pool.

6 Barcelona paid £18m for him in 2003 and he is contracted until 2010. But he has a release clause that says he can leave if Barca receive an offer of £85m!

7 Ronny has been made into a comic book star. In it, he wears the colours of the Brazilian flag, with a yellow shirt, green shorts, white socks and blue shorts. The character also wears a chain with a letter "R" like the one he sports in real life.

8 He is the highest paid footballer in the world, trousering a cool £16m in wages every year!

9 Ronny puts his amazing talent down to a love of music: "I play football with melodies in my head. I listen to dance music all day and take those sounds with me on to the field. That makes me happy, and the happier I am, the easier I play."

10 After Brazil's World Cup exit some crazy fans burned and destroyed a 7.5-metre tall fibreglass and resin statue of Ronaldinho in the Brazilian city of Chapeco. The statue had been erected in 2004 to celebrate his first election as FIFA World Player of the Year...

1

2

4

7

THE PLAY

MARLON HAREWOOD

BORN: Hampstead, London, August 25, 1979
POSITION: Striker **NICKNAME:** Vicehead

CLUBS: Nottingham Forest, Ipswich Town (loan), West Ham.
CAR: Audi. **FAVE MEAL?** Barbecue chicken.
FAVE TV PROGRAMME? *"Smallville."*
BEST MOMENT IN FOOTBALL? "My hat-trick against Aston Villa last season. I was more worried about the team winning than me scoring, but I was on a high for days afterwards."
WORST MOMENT? "When I was on loan at Ipswich, our keeper took a goal-kick and the ball bounced in front – and over – the opposition defence. There was an open net but I was looking at the post and ball at the same time and missed the ball."
BEST PLAYER FACED:? "Tony Adams and Martin Keown when I made my Premiership debut for Forest. I was so scared!"
HAS THE BOSS EVER TOLD YOU OFF? "Not really, I'm a good lad."
IF YOU WEREN'T A FOOTBALLER? "Haven't got a Scooby Doo! I'm working on it, don't worry."
YOUR TEAM-MATE HAS HIT A GOAL-BOUND SHOT. DO YOU GET A TOUCH SO YOU CAN CLAIM A GOAL? "Errrm (laughs)...depends how the ball is, where it was heading. Nah, I'd leave it..."

MAIK TAYLOR

BORN: Hildesheim, Germany, September 4, 1971
POSITION: Goalkeeper **NICKNAME:** Maiky

CLUBS: Barnet, Southampton, Fulham, Birmingham.
CAR: BMW 650. **FAVE MEAL?** "Pasta with chicken."
FAVE TV PROGRAMME? *"They Think It's All Over."*
BEST MOMENT IN FOOTBALL? "Beating England with Northern Ireland. We were the underdogs and it was a proper giant-killing."
WORST MOMENT? "Blackburn away – the last game of the 2001-02 season. I was at Fulham and hadn't played all season but got brought in for that match. We lost 3-0 and the first goal was my mistake. Gutted!"
BEST PLAYER FACED? "Alan Shearer. He had everything, one of the best there's ever been."
IF YOU WEREN'T A FOOTBALLER? "I used to be in the army so I'd probably still be doing that."
YOU'RE PLAYING A MATE'S TEAM AND HE ASKS WHICH OF YOUR PLAYERS ARE INJURED. WHAT DO YOU SAY? "I can't talk right now – I'll give you a ring back at quarter to five on Saturday!"

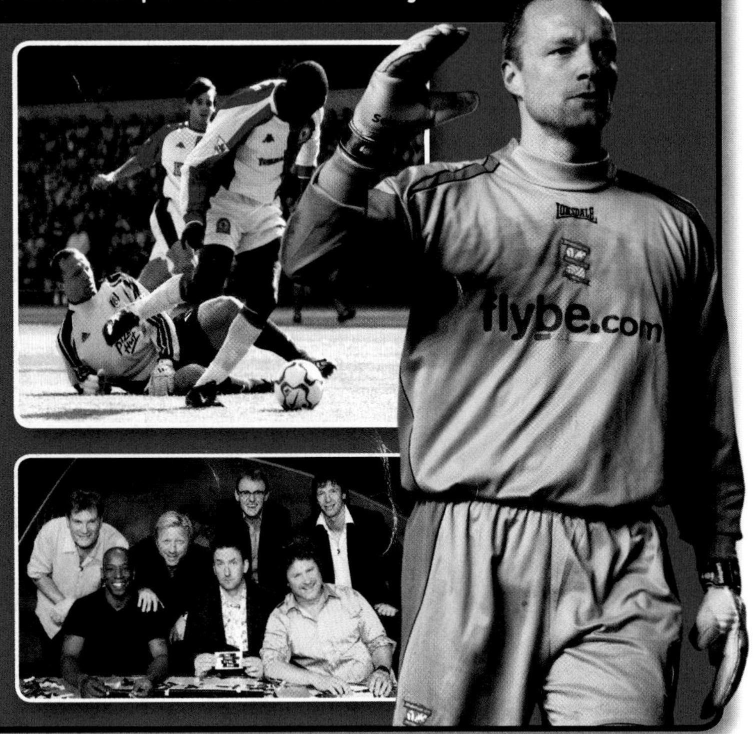

ERFILES!

LOMANA LUA LUA

BORN: December 12, 1980, DR Congo
POSITION: Striker **NICKNAME:** Louie

CLUBS: Colchester, Newcastle United, Portsmouth.
CAR: Range Rover. **FAVE MEAL:** "Chicken, I could eat it every day."
FAVE TV PROGRAMME: "*Takeshi's Castle*."
BEST MOMENT IN FOOTBALL? "Helping Portsmouth stay up last season when it looked unlikely at one point. Also helping DR Congo to the quarter-finals of the African Cup of Nations."
WORST MOMENT? "The death of my son earlier in the year."
BEST PLAYER FACED: "Sol Campbell. Not only is he quick, but he's very strong with it."
IF YOU WEREN'T A FOOTBALLER? "Only God can answer that question, but when I was back home in Congo, I wanted to be a gymnast."
THE BOSS THREATENS TO FINE YOU £1,000 EVERY TIME YOU DO ONE OF YOU FAMOUS BACK-FLIPS. WOULD YOU STOP? "No. Everyone knows me for my back-flips, although I got injured last year. If it is still a bit dangerous, I'll stop altogether, but if everything feels okay then I'll carry on."

LIAM RIDGEWELL

BORN: Bexleyheath, Kent, July 21, 1984
POSITION: Central defender **NICKNAME:** Ridgy

CLUBS: Villa since trainee.
CAR: BMW645. **FAVE MEAL:** "Chicken Tikka Massala."
FAVE TV PROGRAMME: "*Only Fools and Horses*."
BEST MOMENT IN FOOTBALL? "Scoring two goals against Fulham to help us draw 3-3, the day after the birth of my son Luca. That was an unbelievable 24 hours."
WORST MOMENT? "Damaging my medial ligament pre-season. I was out for two-and-a-half months."
BEST PLAYER FACED: "Ruud van Nistelrooy. His movement is amazing, it's terrible trying to pick him up or work out where he is going."
IF YOU WEREN'T A FOOTBALLER? "Something to do with sport, maybe in a leisure centre."
YOU ARE LEAVING TRAINING WHEN YOU SPOT A £50 NOTE IN THE CAR PARK. WHAT WOULD YOU DO? "Pick it up, put it in my wallet and probably spend it on a nice meal out."

THE RISE AND RISE OF PETER CROUCH

PETER'S LONG ROUTE TO THE TOP...

Spurs
Peter was with Spurs as a youth player between 1998 and 2000, but failed to make the grade. He was loaned out to Swedish side IFK Hassleholm where he scored three in eight games, but was then allowed to join QPR.

QPR
Ten goals in 42 games during season 2000-01 didn't set the world alight but he showed enough promise for Portsmouth to pay £1.25m for him when Rangers were relegated.

Portsmouth
With 18 goals in 37 games, Peter had produced the kind of form that gets managers drooling. After less than one season at Fratton Park he was on his way to Villa for £5m in March 2002.

Aston Villa
Scored the equaliser against Newcastle on his home debut, but couldn't get a regular place in the side. He went on loan to Norwich but returned to hit two more in vital games. Peter's tally of six in 37 games didn't impress David O'Leary.

FACT
Peter, born in Macclesfield, Cheshire, on January 31, 1981, was a QPR fan and became a ball boy at the age of ten when his family moved back to London after spending a year in Singapore.

PETER CROUCH took a long while to get there, but the Premiership's tallest player is now a key man for England.

After seven clubs in just six years, Crouchy finally made the massive move to Liverpool in July 2005. But even that looked as though it was a big mistake when he went 19 games without scoring.

But the 6ft 7in star isn't one to give up easily and once he'd scored his first goal he was on his way.

Crouchy won over The Kop with his determination and self-less teamwork but then he had to get England supporters on his side.

Booed by fans when he came on at Old Trafford as a sub during the 2-1 World Cup qualifier against Poland, he turned the jeers to cheers before the finals. March 2006 brought his first England goal, including a hat-trick in the 6-0 rout of Jamaica at Old Trafford.

Do the Robokop!

PETER SAYS HE is ditching his Robokop celebration. **Shoot** says: "Bring it back!" The whole nation warmed to Peter's goal-scoring dance which began at the Beckhams' pre-World Cup bash and developed during the following friendlies.

But Crouchy binned his celebration and said he wouldn't strut his stuff unless England won the World Cup: "It's not about robotic dancing. It is about scoring goals and winning matches."
His England team-mates said he should get grooving. And so do we...

Norwich City

Crouchy was a big hit during his loan spell at Carrow Road when he scored four in 15 games. The Canaries wanted to keep him after his three-month loan between September and December 2003 and even gave him a Championship medal.

Southampton

In July 2004, Peter headed back to the South Coast when Southampton forked out £2m for his services. Despite his 16 goals in 33 appearances, Saints were relegated and exactly a year later he was on the move yet again.

Liverpool

The £7m The Reds paid for Peter looked like money wasted as he went 19 games before he scored his first goal. And that strike against Wigan was only awarded after an appeal. Five goals in December won over the fans and his first season at Anfield produced a total of eight over 32 games.

England

Peter has been part of the England set-up since 1999 and has appeared for the Youth and Under-21 sides. But he had to wait until May 2005 for his senior call-up. He then scored six in his first ten games and hit the World Cup opener against Trinidad & Tobago.

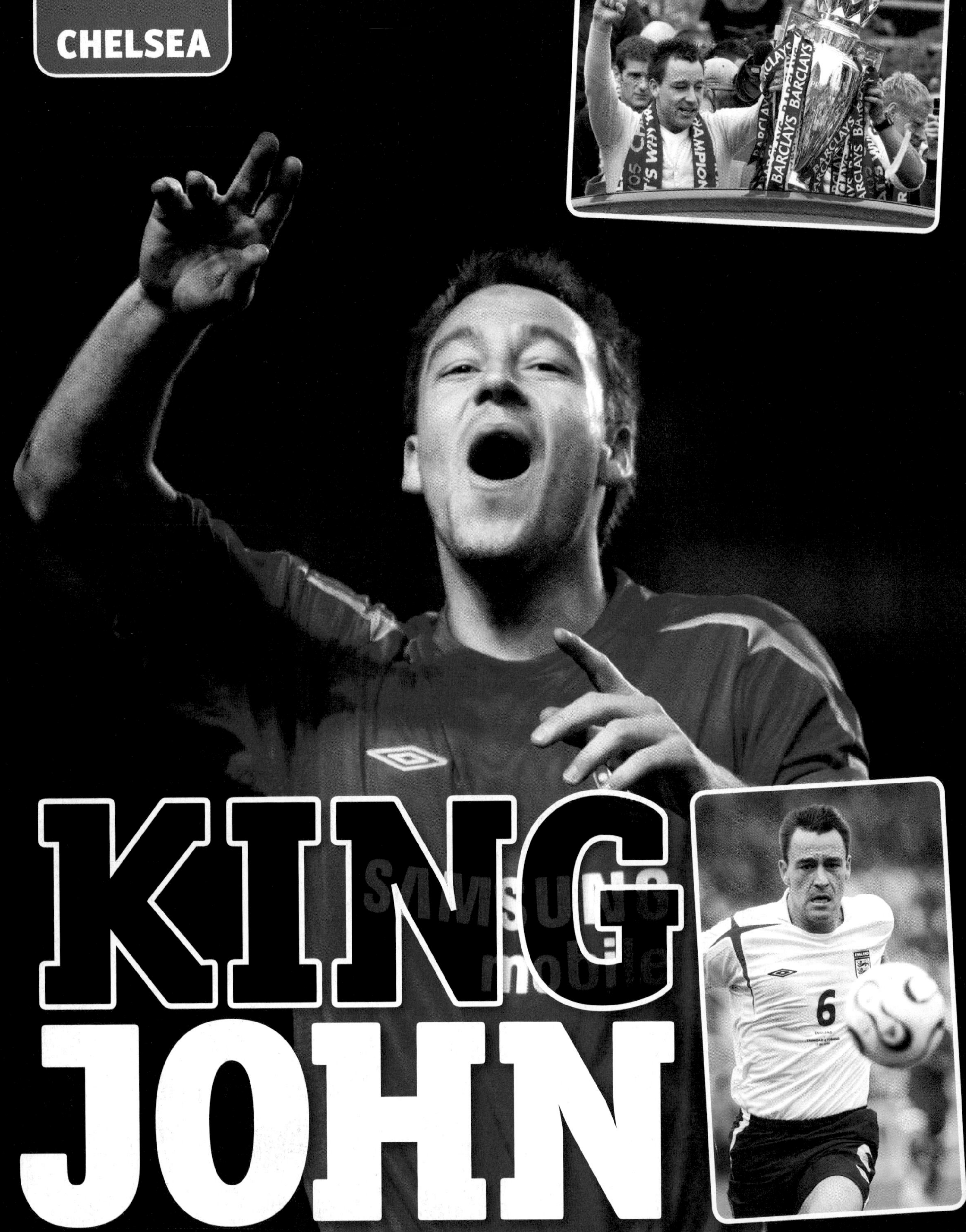

KING JOHN

He's a defensive rock for club and country. The man you would want by your side in battle. Meet the King of Stamford Bridge, the bravest of the Lions... John Terry!

SIX YEARS AGO John Terry wasn't sure where his career was going. He'd been out on loan to Nottingham Forest for two months and only had a handful of appearances under his belt for Chelsea.

But his six games at the City Ground proved to be time well spent. Less than three years after his return to Stamford Bridge he was a first-team regular and in the England side.

Former boss Claudio Ranieri first handed him the captain's armband in 2003-04, but only when injury kept French legend Marcel Desailly out of the side. The arrival of new boss Jose Mourinho in June 2004 saw John take over as skipper for the following season after the retirement of Desailly, a player JT credits with helping his development.

To back his coach's support, John earned the PFA Player of the Year award; won a place in a World XI chosen by footballers from 40 countries; and was voted the best defender in the Champions League 2005. He admits: "I have been here since I was 14 and I would love to stay at Chelsea for the rest of my career. I love playing for the club."

And if you still need convincing about this guy's quality, remember that he was named in FIFA's squad of the tournament despite England having a disappointing World Cup campaign.

10 THINGS YOU SHOULD KNOW ABOUT JOHN TERRY...

1 His older brother Paul plays for Yeovil Town in League One. Paul is married to the sister of West Ham and England defender Paul Konchesky.

2 John is a born winner. He fancies himself at darts, pool and often has PlayStation competitions round his house for the other players.

3 Don't ask him to do keepy-ups! JT hates doing them and reckons he's not that good at juggling balls. Typical no-nonsense defender.

4 May 30, 2006 will be etched forever in John's memory as he scored his first England goal, during the team's 3-1 victory over Hungary (right).

5 He first wore the England captain's armband against Poland in October 2005 when Michael Owen left the pitch. But his biggest thrill was taking over from the substituted David Beckham in the World Cup finals game against Ecuador (right).

6 Many of JT's team-mates are his neighbours in Surrey and Sky Sports' commentator Martin Tyler lives just down the road.

7 John was the first Chelsea skipper in 50 years to lift the league title in 2005. The 2006 win was the club's first back-to-back championship.

8 England kit suppliers Umbro have signed the defender on a deal for "life" to wear and promote their boots. He replaces the retired Alan Shearer who has become their ambassador.

9 John's Chelsea contract will keep him at Stamford Bridge until the summer of 2009, when he will still only be 28.

10 He's already released a book called My Winning Season, but has a deal, thought to be worth around £1m, to produce more publications during the course of his career.

STEVE COPPELL

Many people reckon Steve Coppell bears a striking resemblance to Bono. Judging by the shot on the right, the U2 frontman should be starting to get worried!

STEVE McCLAREN

Fresh-faced Steve McClaren looked the picture of health during his playing days. Guess that's what five years managing Middlesbrough does to a man!

TRADING

GLENN ROEDER

Glenn Roeder was an elegant centre-half but he would never have made it in today's game. All of the current stars would have sorted that barnet by now...

PETER TAYLOR

With Simon Jordan in charge at Selhurst Park, new Crystal Palace manager Peter Taylor will be hoping it's not a case of "hair today, gone tomorrow."

FACES

Check out some of today's managers and players who have suffered at the hands of time...

GEORGE BURLEY

Do you think the pained expression on George Burley's face in the pic on the right is because someone's just shown him the one on the left?!

HENRIK LARSSON

The realisation he was Jar-Jar Binks' double was too much for Henrik Larsson. At least someone has reason to be pleased the Star Wars moves got made!

PAUL LE GUEN

If Paul Le Guen fails as Rangers boss he could always go back to his old day job - posing for police photofits! Come on Paul, give us a smile!...!

TEDDY SHERINGHAM

Teddy Sheringham has been playing for so long that the only surprise to us at Shoot Towers was that the photo from his Millwall days wasn't in black and white!

10 THINGS YOU SHOULD KNOW ABOUT...

THEO WALCOTT

1 Theo was born in Stanmore, London, on March 16, 1989. Unsurprisingly, he was a champion sprinter at school.

2 Theo played for AFC Newbury as a junior (he scored over 100 goals in his one and only season) before joining Southampton where he played 23 games (ten as a sub) and scored five goals.

3 Harry Redknapp, who worked with Theo at Southampton, says: "The kid can run through puddles and not make a splash. He is lightning quick and drifts over the ground."

4 Theo moved to Arsenal as a 16-year-old in January 2006 for an initial £5m. This will rise by a further seven million pounds depending on appearances for club and country.

5 He became England's youngest-ever player aged just 17 years and 75 days when he made his debut as a substitute against Hungary last May.

6 Theo was picked for the World Cup despite NEVER having played in the Premiership — and with Sven Goran Eriksson NEVER having seen him in action, except on video.

7 His girlfriend Melanie Slade is being touted as the next Coleen or Victoria Beckham. But she herself shuns the limelight and says she just wants to be a physiotherapist! Her dad is Southampton's city mayor.

8 Theo's dad has said he is related to a legendary West Indian cricketer: "Sir Clyde Walcott is my dad's cousin and we're quite a sporting family," says Theo. But there appears to be some doubt. As Sir Clyde himself insists: "He may be a very good player, but he's definitely not a relative. In fact, I don't even know who he is."

9 Wayne Rooney is a big fan, saying: "He is better than I was at that age."

10 Although he didn't get the gig at this year's World Cup, never fear – he's in good company! Ronaldo sat out the whole of the 1994 tournament but then went on to become the highest-ever goalscorer in the World Cup.

4

WALCOTT 32

5

7

8

KNOW YOUR FOOTBALL?

Find out if you are a footie mastermind with our great quiz and super crossword!

CELEBRITYFANS

Which clubs do the following people support...?

A. Tony Blair **B. Perry Fenwick** **C.** Prince William

TRUEORFALSE

Identify which of these statements are true or false.

1. Robbie Fowler is Liverpool's leading goal scorer of all-time.

2. Arsenal manager Arsene Wenger was in the French team that won the 1984 European Championships.

3. Hearts won last season's Scottish FA Cup.

TRIVIAL TEAZERS

1. Against which team did Wayne Rooney make his World Cup finals debut in the summer?

2. Who is the former England defender who succeeded Steve McClaren as manager of Middlesbrough?

3. Who won last season's Championship play-off final by defeating Leeds United 3-0 at the Millennium Stadium?

4. Shay Given, Alan Shearer and David Batty have all played for which two Premiership clubs?

5. Which Championship club plays at the Kingston Communications Stadium?

6. Who scored two goals in last season's FA Cup Final?

7. Which two London clubs competed in this season's UEFA Cup?

8. Osasuna qualified for the Champions League by finishing fourth in which country last season?

9. Which Premiership club are nicknamed "The Latics"?

10. Who became Manchester United captain after Roy Keane moved to Celtic in December 2005?

FOOTIE CROSSWORD

CLUES ACROSS

1 - - - Quinn, former Sunderland and Republic of Ireland striker (5)

4 See 1 Down

6 Irish full-back, Stephen, who joined Newcastle from Tottenham in 2003 (4)

10 - - - Ameobi, striker who partnered Alan Shearer in his last season at St. James' Park (5)

11 Port Vale boss, Martin - - - (5)

12 Kit Kat Crescent Conference club unable to reclaim a League Two spot (4)

13 England World Cup striker, - - - Crouch (5)

14 See 32 Across

17 Steve Coppell's Royals – Premiership new boys (7)

18 Luis Felipe, Portugal's Brazilian coach who turned down the England job (7)

19 Man City forward, Darius, twice on target against old club Villa last season (7)

22 Nickname associated with England's 2006 European Champions League finalists (7)

24 - - - van Nistelrooy, Man United's leading scorer last season (4)

25 Norwich City left-back and former skipper, Adam (5)

26 Andy, ex-Forest winger whose Spurs season was hit by injury (4)

30 Old Liverpool skipper, - - - Hughes, who passed away in 2004 (5)

31 Micky, manager who steered Coventry into the top half of The Championship in 2006 (5)

32 & 14 Bayview Stadium club from Scotland's Third Division (4,4)

33 Andy, captain prominent in Blackburn's push for a UEFA Cup slot (4)

34 The Blades' promotion-winning keeper, Paddy (5)

CLUES DOWN

1 & 4 Across Former Man United, Newcastle and England midfielder relegated with Birmingham (5,4)

2 Homeland of Wigan defender, Paul Scharner (7)

3 French club guided to the 2006 title by boss Gerard Houllier (4)

4 Holland midfielder, George - part of Boro's 2006 UEFA Cup Final team (7)

5 Nickname of Premiership club from Goodison (7)

7 United States of - - -, Brad Friedel's World Cup contenders (7)

8 Nickname of the 2006 Carling Cup winners (3,6)

9 Scotland's Somerset Park club managed last term by Robert Connor (3)

15 Robert, former Arsenal winger now at Villarreal (5)

16 Luke, Charlton and England right-back (5)

17 The - - - Stadium, home of Middlesbrough (9)

20 Graeme, manager sacked by Newcastle in February (7)

21 Blackburn's long-injured Italian, - - - Amoruso, released in May (7)

22 Stevie, 2006 PFA Player of the Year (7)

23 Brazilian midfielder in the Juventus team beaten by Arsenal in last season's Champions League (7)

27 - - - Murphy, midfield man who joined Tottenham from Charlton in 2005 (5)

28 - - - Trafford, stadium known as the Theatre of Dreams (3)

29 Man United's South Korean star, Ji-Sung (4)

Answers on page 110

onelove

PHOTOGRAPHER LEVON BISS was given a job many football fans dream about – he was told to go off around the world shooting pictures of our favourite game.

England stars Michael Owen, John Terry and David James, Liverpool midfielder Luis Garcia, Barcelona playmaker Deco, plus Newcastle striker Shola Ameobi and his former skipper Alan Shearer were just a few of the players captured by Levon's lenses.

The London-based snapper was commissioned to compile a special book of photographs by Umbro for their "One Love" campaign. Levon jetted all over the planet to create the book and a special exhibition of his work which aimed to portray football from grassroots through to the top professional clubs. We asked some of the stars to pick out their favourite pictures and tell us about them...

TIM CAHILL EVERTON & AUSTRALIA

Lifeguards playing on Scarborough Beach, Perth, Australia

"As an Australian, I'd have to say this is my favourite image," said Tim. "It's the perfect scene – on the beach, playing a bit of footie with your mates then hitting the surf!"

LEVON BISS PHOTOGRAPHER

Fans celebrate after a Black Leopards goal in Makhado, South Africa

"The reason for choosing this image is because it illustrates the passion and intensity of the many people I met during the project. Love for the game of football unites diverse people across the globe and this shot epitomizes that," said Levon.

JOHN TERRY CHELSEA & ENGLAND

Duthni, South Africa

"This is my favourite because it shows the innocence of the game," said the Stamford Bridge skipper. "I think these days there's the potential for kids to be coached out of their enjoyment. It's important for kids at a grassroots level to make sure they enjoy the game."

MICHAEL OWEN NEWCASTLE & ENGLAND

Groundsman at Universitario De Deportes Stadiu, Arequipa, Peru

It looks like the stadium is packed to bursting point with supporters, but in reality the seats have been painted to give the effect that they are all full. "Sunderland could do with some of that," joked Michael, who features in the book working out in the gym as he battled back from his broken foot.

SHOLA AMEOBI NEWCASTLE & ENGLAND

Over-65 women's football, Thohoyandou University, South Africa

"What drew me to this picture was the vibrantly coloured clothes the women are wearing," said Shola. "I later learnt they belong to a local tribe, and the tribes form teams to play in leagues as part of a government scheme to promote healthy living among the elderly."

SHOOT MONTHLY

LET US TAKE YOU AROUND THE CLUBS

Your fantastic bumper guide to all the clubs – from the Premiership right down to League Two!

All you need to know about... THE GUNNERS

The History

Founded at the Government's arms factory in South London in 1886, they moved north of the Thames in 1913. Previously known as Dial Square, Royal Arsenal and Woolwich Arsenal.
Address: Emirates Stadium, Ashburton Grove, London N1.
Ground capacity: 60,000.
Club Tel: 0207 704 4000.
Ticket Office: 0207 704 4040.

Arsenal Legends

1980s Tony Adams
(1984-2002) Tony (above) lifted nine trophies during his 668 games. Appointed as their youngest skipper in 1988, aged 21. Set up a clinic to help people with addiction problems.
1990s Ian Wright
(1991-1998) The club's record scorer until his tally of 185 was overtaken by Henry last year. Ian (above) is now a TV celeb.

2000s Thierry Henry
(1999-present) Arguably the deadliest forward in the world at the moment with blistering speed and incredible skill.

Club Honours

Premiership Champions: 1998, 2002, 2004 (below).

Division One: 1931, 1933, 1934, 1935, 1938, 1948, 1953, 1971, 1989, 1991.
FA Cup: 1930, 1936, 1950, 1971, 1979, 1993, 1998, 2002, 2003.
League Cup: 1987, 1993.
UEFA Cup: 1970 (Fairs Cup),
Cup Winners' Cup: 1994.

Record transfers

In: £13m to Bordeaux for Sylvain Wiltord, August 2000.
Out: £23.5m from Real Madrid for Nicolas Anelka (left), August 1999.

Young star

Spain midfielder Cesc Fabregas (below) became the club's youngest-ever Premiership player when he took to the pitch against Everton in August 2004 at the age of 17 years and 103 days. Last season he played 50 games and earned a World Cup call-up.

Did you know?

The new Emirates Stadium, built at a cost of £390m, and just a long free-kick away from Highbury, is actually Arsenal's seventh ground since they were formed.

Season 2005-06

Premiership: 4th.
Champions League: Beaten finalists.
Top scorer: Thierry Henry, 33.
Player of the Year: Thierry Henry.

Arsenal
★ STAR PLAYER ★
THIERRY HENRY
BORN: August 17, 1977, Paris.
HEIGHT: 6ft 2in. WEIGHT: 13st 5lb.
PREVIOUS CLUBS: Monaco, Juventus.
DID YOU KNOW? In 2005-06, Thierry became the first player to score more than 20 goals in five consecutive seasons, earning four Golden Boots along the way.

★ STAR PLAYER ★
STEVEN DAVIS

BORN: January 1, 1985, Ballymena.
HEIGHT: 5ft 7in. **WEIGHT:** 9st 7lb.
PREVIOUS CLUBS: Villa from trainee.
DID YOU KNOW? Man United scouts recently eyed Steven up as a possible replacement for Roy Keane, but Villa stepped in with a new long-term deal.

All you need to know about... THE VILLANS

The History
Started life in 1874 when a local church cricket club decided there weren't enough football clubs in the Aston area of Birmingham.
Address: Villa Park, Birmingham B6 6HE.
Ground capacity: 42,500.
Club Tel: 0121 322 2107.
Ticket Off: 0121 327 5353.

Villa Legends

1980s Peter Withe
(1980-85) The striker (above) became the club's record signing when he joined from Nottingham Forest for £500,000. Hit 20 goals as Villa won the tile in his first season and scored the European Cup winner against Bayern in 1982.
1990s Paul McGrath
(1989-96) Nicknamed "God" by the Villa fans, the tough

tackling Republic of Ireland defender (above) was the PFA Player of the Year in 1993.
2000s Gareth Barry
(1997-present) Gareth (below) made his Villa debut at 18, after a move from Brighton. Can play in defence or midfield. Record 27 starts for England Under-21s.

Club Honours
Division One: 1894, 1896, 1897, 1899, 1900, 1910, 1981.

Division Two: 1938, 1960.
Division Three: 1972.
FA Cup: 1887, 1895, 1897, 1905, 1913, 1920, 1957.
League Cup: 1961, 1975, 1977, 1994, 1996.
European Cup: 1982 (above).
European Super Cup: 1983.

Record transfers
In: £9.5m to River Plate, for Juan Pablo Angel (right), January 2001.
Out: £12.6m from Man United for Dwight Yorke, August 1998.

Young star
England Under-21 defender Liam Ridgewell (below) began his career with West Ham but was 16 when he moved to Villa. Less than a year later he had won the FA Youth Cup and is now a valued member of the first-team squad.

Did you know?
Nigel Spink had played just one game for Villa when he came off the bench as the sub keeper to help them win the European Cup in 1982.

Season 2005-06
Premiership: 16th.
Top scorer: Milan Baros, 12.
Player of the Year: Steven Davis.

All you need to know about... THE ROVERS

The History

Founded in 1875 by a group of public schoolboys, led by John Lewis, a founder of the Lancashire FA who was also a referee at two FA Cup Finals.
Address: Ewood Park, Blackburn BB2 4JF.
Ground capacity: 31,367.
Club Tel: 0870 111 3232.
Ticket Office: 0870 112 3456.

Blackburn Legends

1980s Simon Garner
(1978–1992) Fans still sing his name despite him leaving the club 14 years ago. Simon

(above) is Rovers' record scorer with 168 goals in 455 games.
1990s Alan Shearer
(1992-96) Yes, before he struck gold with home-town club Newcastle, Big Al (above right) knocked in 112 goals

in 138 games for Rovers and helped them to the Premiership title in 1995.
2000s Brad Friedel
(2001-present) Commanding and consistent, the 82-cap United States keeper (below) is regarded as one of the Premiership's best.

Club Honours

Premiership: 1995 (below).

Division One: 1912, 1914.
Division Two: 1939.
Division Three: 1975.
FA Cup: 1884, 1885, 1886, 1890, 1891, 1928.
League Cup: 2002.

Record transfers

In: £7.5m to Man United for Andy Cole, December (right) 2001.
Out: £16m from Chelsea for Damien Duff, July 2003.

Young star

Eddie Nolan (below), a Republic of Ireland Under-19 defender who earned a first-team squad number after sterling displays for the reserves.

Did you know?

Blackburn, backed by local businessman and fan Jack Walker, were founder members of the Premiership in 1992. Runners-up to Manchester United in 1994, they won the title the following year.

Season 2005-06

Premiership: 6th
Top scorer: Craig Bellamy, 17.
Player of the Year: Craig Bellamy.

BORN: October 18, 1974, Wrexham.
HEIGHT: 5ft 11in. **WEIGHT:** 11st.
PREVIOUS CLUBS: Manchester United, Crewe, Leicester City, Birmingham City
DID YOU KNOW? Robbie joined Rovers to be near his parents in Wrexham, but he's further away than when at Birmingham.

BORN: September 25, 1978, Jamaica.
HEIGHT: 5ft 9in. **WEIGHT:** 11st.
PREVIOUS CLUBS: Harbour View.
DID YOU KNOW? Wanderers paid £1m for Ricardo after spotting him at the 1998 World Cup finals. He made his debut for Harbour View at the age of just 14.

All you need to know about... THE TROTTERS

The History
Began life as Christ Church Sunday School club in 1874, but broke away and became Wanderers three years later.
Address: Reebok Stadium, Burnden Way, Lostock, Bolton BL6 6JW.
Ground capacity: 27,879.
Club Tel: 01204 673 673.
Ticket Off: 0871 871 2932.

Bolton Legends
1980s Brian Kidd

(1980-82) The former Man United striker (above) made just 43 appearances but his 14 goals won over the fans.
1990s John McGinlay
(1992-1997) John's goals during season 1996–97 ensured Bolton stayed in the Premiership. The Scottish star

(above) and Nathan Blake hit 54 to give Wanderers the First Division title with a record 98 points and 100 goals.
2000s Kevin Nolan
(1999-present) Kevin (below)

made his Bolton debut at 17 and was captain by the age of 23. An attacking midfielder with a knack for scoring goals, he can also play in defence. Expected to star for England.

Club Honours
Division One: 1997.
Division Two: 1909, 1978.
Division Three: 1973.
FA Cup: 1923, 1926, 1929, 1958 (below).

Record transfers
In: £3.5m to Wimbledon for Dean Holdsworth, October 1997.
Out: £4.5m from Liverpool for Jason McAteer, (below left) September 1995.

Young star
Signed from Farense in August 2003, Portuguese striker Ricardo Vaz Te (below) can also play wide. Has the ability to beat players and strike sensational shots.

Did you know?
Bolton and England keeper Dick Pym won the FA Cup Final in 1923, 1926 and 1929, and never conceded a goal at Wembley.

Season 2005-06
Premiership: 8th.
Top scorer: Stelios Giannakopoulos 12.
Player of the Year: Ricardo Gardner.

All you need to know about... THE ADDICKS

The History

Originally a group of 14 and 15-year-olds based in the Greenwich area whose results in local leagues were so good they turned professional in 1920 and joined the Football League a year later.
Address: The Valley, Floyd Rd, Charlton, London SE7 8BL.
Ground capacity: 27,111.
Club Tel: 0208 333 4000.
Ticket Off: 0871 226 1905.

Charlton Legends

1980s Derek Hales
(1973-1976, 1978-1985)
Record goalscorer (above) with 168 in 320 games in two spells at the club. Lethal in the area and formed a great partnership with Mike Flanagan.
1990s Clive Mendonca
(1997-1999) A knee injury forced Clive's early retirement,

but not before 40 goals in just 84 games, including the first Premiership hat-trick at The Valley (v Southampton). Clive (above) also registered a treble against Sunderland in a play-off final victory.
2000s Chris Powell
(1998-2003, 2005-2006)

Charlton's most-capped England player with five to his name, Chris (below left) is a dependable left-back. Had two successful spells before joining Watford.

Club Honours

Division One: 2000 (below).

Division Three (S): 1929, 1935.
FA Cup: 1947.

Record transfers

In: £4.75m to Wimbledon for striker Jason Euell in July 2001.
Out: £10m from Chelsea for midfielder Scott Parker (right) in January 2004.

Young star

Injuries have hampered left-back Nathan Ashton (below) who has worked his way through Charlton's academy to England Under-18s and 19s.

Did you know?

Charlton, then a Division Two side, signed former European Footballer of the Year Allan Simonsen in 1982. He is the only player to have scored in the European Cup, UEFA Cup and Cup Winners' Cup finals.

Season 2005-06

Premiership: 13th.
Top scorer: Darren Bent, 22.
Player of the Year: Darren Bent.

CHARLTON ATHLETIC

BORN: March 23, 1983, Brent, London.
HEIGHT: 5ft 9in. **WEIGHT:** 11st 9lb.
PREVIOUS CLUBS: Luton Town, Arsenal, QPR (loan).
DID YOU KNOW? The England Youth and Under-20 left winger cost The Addicks £100,000 from Arsenal in February 2004.

CHELSEA
FOOTBALL CLUB
SAMSUNG
mobile
★ STAR PLAYER ★
FRANK LAMPARD
BORN: June 20, 1978, Romford, Essex.
HEIGHT: 6ft. WEIGHT: 14st 1lb.
PREVIOUS CLUBS: West Ham United, Swansea City (loan).
DID YOU KNOW? The Football Writers' Footballer of the Year was runner-up to Ronaldinho in both the European and World Player of the Year awards.

All you need to know about... THE BLUES

The History

Formed in 1905 when Fulham turned down the chance to rent Stamford Bridge, they were immediately allowed to join League Division Two.

Address: Stamford Bridge, Fulham Rd, London SW6 1HS.

Ground capacity: 42,522.

Club Tel: 0870 300 1212.

Ticket Off: 0870 300 2322.

Chelsea Legends

1980s Kerry Dixon (1983-1992) Bought from Reading for £175,000, Kerry (above) was good in the air and could use both feet. Scored 147 league goals in 335 games and reached double-figures in all but one of his seasons at The Bridge before being sold to Southampton for £575,000.

1990s Gianfranco Zola (1996–2003) Football Writers'

Footballer of the Year in 1997, Franco (above) was the only person to receive the award without playing a whole season. Helped The Blues win the League Cup, European Cup Winners' Cup and Super Cup in 1998 and the FA Cup in 1997 and 2000.

2000s John Terry (1998–present) JT (below) is

captain at The Bridge and destined to be skipper of England. A product of the Chelsea youth set-up who kick-started his career with a loan to Nottingham Forest.

Club Honours

Premiership: 2005, 2006 (below).

Division One: 1955.
Division Two: 1984, 1989.
FA Cup: 1970, 1997, 2000.
League Cup: 1965, 1998, 2005.
Cup Winners' Cup: 1971, 1998.
Super Cup: 1999.

Record transfers

In: £30m to AC Milan for Andriy Shevchenko (right), May 2006.

Out: £12m from Rangers for Tor Andre Flo, November 2000.

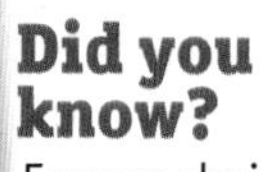

Young star

Defensive midfielder Lassana Diarra (below) signed from Le Havre in summer 2005 and is touted as the new Makelele.

Did you know?

Former chairman Ken Bates (left) bought the club for just £1 in 1982. He reportedly made £17m when he sold to Roman Abramovich in July 2003.

Season 2005-06

Premiership: Champions.
Champions League: Second round.
Top scorer: Frank Lampard, 20.
Player of the Year: John Terry.

All you need to know about... THE TOFFEES

The History

The team began life in 1878 as St. Domingo Church Sunday School and changed their name to Everton a year later. They played in Stanley Park.

Address: Goodison Park, Goodison Rd, Liverpool L4 4EL.
Ground capacity: 40,565.
Club Tel: : 0151 330 2200.
Ticket Off: 0870 442 1878.

Everton Legends

1980s Neville Southall (1981-1997) Once regarded as the best keeper in the world, Big Nev (below) played

a record 578 League games for Everton, 750 in all, and won 92 caps playing for Wales.

1990s Duncan Ferguson (1994-1998, 2000-06) The giant striker has the Everton club crest tattooed on his body.

A former Rangers and Scotland star, Duncan (above) won the FA Cup with The Toffees in 1995.

2000s Tim Cahill (2004-present) A £2m buy from Millwall, midfielder Tim (below) won Australia's first-

ever World Cup Man of the Match award at Germany 06.

Club Honours

Division One: 1891, 1915, 1928, 1932, 1939, 1963, 1970, 1985, 1987.
Division Two: 1931.
FA Cup: 1906, 1933, 1966, 1984, 1995.
Cup Winners' Cup: 1985 (below).

Record transfers

In: £8.6m to Crystal Palace for Andrew Johnson, June 2006.
Out: £30m from Man United for Wayne Rooney (above), August 2004.

Young star

James Vaughan was Everton's youngest-ever player when he made his first-team debut in April 2005. The striker became the club's, and Premiership's, youngest scorer in that match against Palace, at the age of 16 years and 271 days.

Did you know?

Everton's worst-ever start to a season was in 1994-95 when they failed to win until their 13th League game.

Season 2005-06

Premiership: 11th.
Top scorer: James Beattie, 11.
Player of the Year: Mikel Arteta (below).

★ STAR PLAYER ★

JAMES BEATTIE

BORN: February 27, 1978, Lancaster.
HEIGHT: 6ft 1in. **WEIGHT:** 13st 6lb.
PREVIOUS CLUBS: Blackburn Rovers, Southampton.
DID YOU KNOW? As a junior swimmer, he was ranked second in the country at 100m freestyle, until a shoulder injury.

BORN: July 9, 1984, Wandsworth.
HEIGHT: 5ft 9in **WEIGHT:** 11st 5lb.
PREVIOUS CLUBS: Bristol City, Torquay United (loan).
DID YOU KNOW? Liam's dad is former West Ham striker Leroy, ex-boss of Torquay and now in charge at Brentford.

All you need to know about... THE COTTAGERS

The History

Fulham St. Andrew's Church Sunday School FC was formed in 1879 and became Fulham in 1888. The oldest professional team in the capital.

Address: Craven Cottage, Stevenage Rd, London SW6 6HH

Ground capacity: 22,230.

Club Tel: 0870 442 1222.

Ticket Off: 0870 442 1234.

Fulham Legends

1980s Gordon Davies (1978-84; 1986-1991) The Wales star (above) is the club's record league scorer with 159, 180 in all. Also their leading hitman in the top-flight with 24 in the old Division One in 1982.

1990s Simon Morgan (1990-2001) Promotion-winning skipper in 1996-97, Simon

(above) is now in charge of their community scheme. Known as "Mr Fulham" after making more than 400 appearances.

2000s Collins John (2004-present) Liberian-born

Holland striker who joined Fulham as a 19-year-old in January 2004 from FC Twente. Collins (below left) scored 11 goals in 37 matches last year, but started only 15 times.

Club Honours

Division One: 2001 (below).

Division Two: 1949, 1999

Division Three (S): 1932.

Record transfers

In: £11.5m to Lyon for Steve Marlet (right), August 2001.

Out: £11.5m from Man United for Louis Saha, January 2004.

Young star

Paris-born striker Ismael Ehui (below) moved to London with his parents and was spotted by the club's scouts. He's been a major success in the Under-17

and Under-19 sides and his prolific goal-scoring has seen him likened to Ian Wright.

Did you know?

The attendance at last year's 1-0 win over bitter local rivals Chelsea was 22,486. If you are thinking that's above the ground capacity – the extra 256 people watched the game from executive boxes.

Season 2005-06

Premiership: 12th.

Top scorer: Collins John, 12.

Player of the Year: Brian McBride.

YOU'LL NEVER WALK ALONE

All you need to know about... THE REDS

The History
Founded when Everton split into two teams in 1892 following a dispute with their landlord. The clubs still play on opposite sides of Stanley Park.
Address: Anfield, Anfield Road, Liverpool L4 0TH.
Ground capacity: 45,360.
Club Tel: 0151 263 2361.
Ticket Off: 0870 220 2345.

Red Legends
1980s Ian Rush

(1980-1987, 1988-1996) The club's record scorer (above) with a staggering 346 goals in 658 appearances for The Reds.
1990s Robbie Fowler
(1991-2001, 2006-present) Local lad Robbie (above right) scored 120 goals in 236 League games during his first spell at Anfield.

2000s Steven Gerrard
(1997-present) Current PFA Player of the Year (below), scorer of the first goal in the Champions League Final comeback against Milan and the man who ruled during last year's FA Cup Final win. Just a few highlights from a player who turned down Chelsea.

Club Honours
Division One: 1901, 1906, 1922, 1923, 1947, 1964, 1966, 1973, 1976, 1977, 1979, 1980, 1982, 1983, 1984, 1986, 1988, 1990.
FA Cup: 1965, 1974, 1986, 1989, 1992, 2001, 2006.
League Cup: 1981, 1982, 1983, 1984, 1995, 2001, 2003.
European Cup: 1977, 1978, 1981, 1984.
Champions League: 2005 (below).

UEFA Cup: 1973, 1976, 2001.
Super Cup: 1977, 2001.

Record transfers
In: £14m to Auxerre for Djibril Cisse (right), July 2004.
Out: £12.5m from Leeds for Robbie Fowler, November 2001.

Young star

Paul Anderson, 18 (above), can play on either wing and was part of the Under-18 team which won the 2006 FA Youth Cup.

Did you know?
Record goal-scorer Ian Rush scored his first Liverpool goal against Arsenal's John Lukic. Twelve years later he scored his 200th for the club, also against Lukic, who had by then moved to Leeds.

Season 2005-06
Premiership: 3rd.
Top scorer: Steven Gerrard, 21.
Player of the Year: Steven Gerrard.

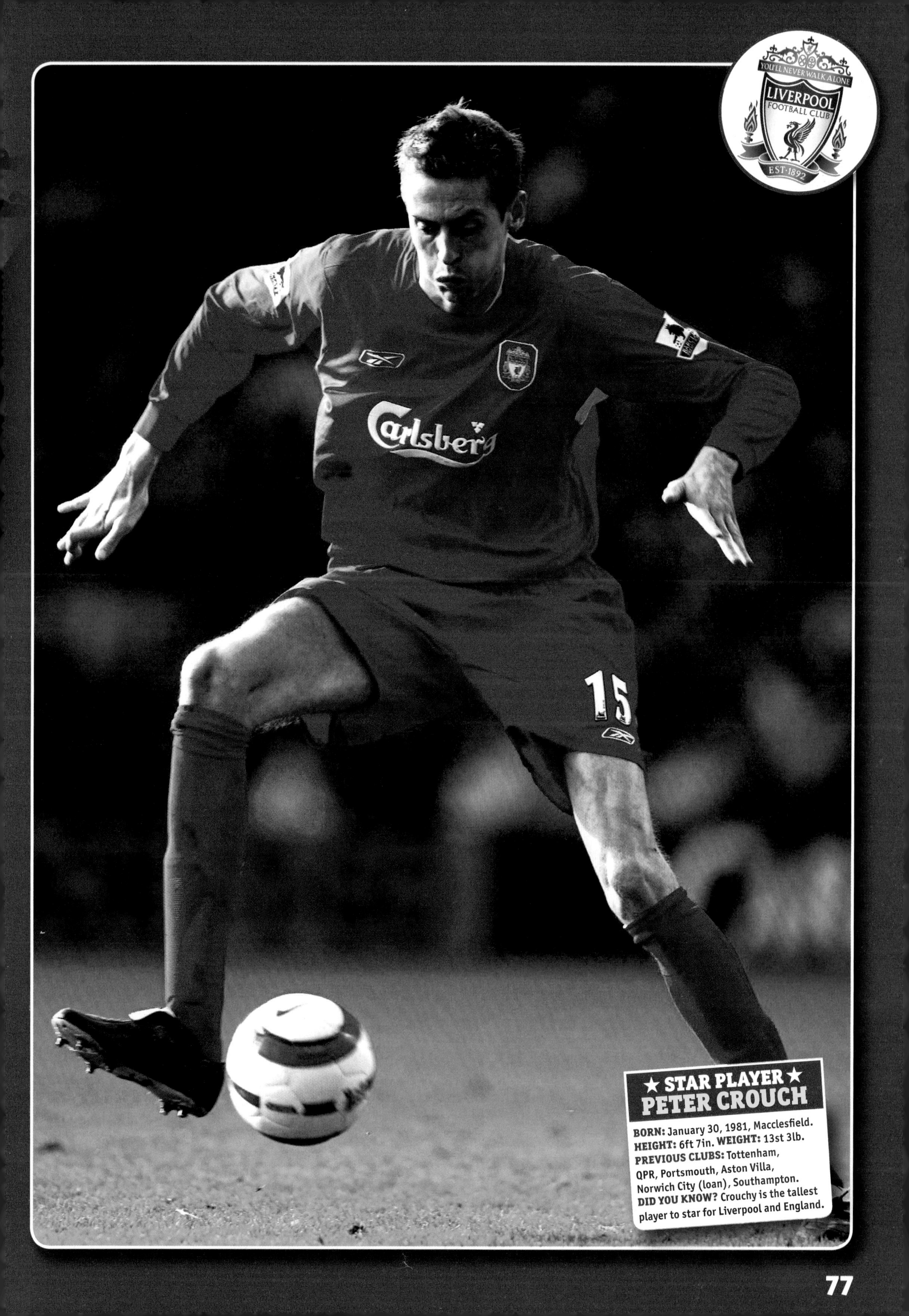

★ STAR PLAYER ★
PETER CROUCH

BORN: January 30, 1981, Macclesfield.
HEIGHT: 6ft 7in. **WEIGHT:** 13st 3lb.
PREVIOUS CLUBS: Tottenham, QPR, Portsmouth, Aston Villa, Norwich City (loan), Southampton.
DID YOU KNOW? Crouchy is the tallest player to star for Liverpool and England.

★ STAR PLAYER ★ RICHARD DUNNE

BORN: September 21, 1979, Dublin.
HEIGHT: 6ft 2in. **WEIGHT:** 15st 12lb.
PREVIOUS CLUBS: Everton.
DID YOU KNOW? He battled back from disciplinary and fitness problems to earn a Republic of Ireland recall and win City's Player of the Year award in 2005-06.

All you need to know about... THE CITIZENS

The History

Originally called Ardwick, the club went bankrupt in 1894 and became Manchester City. As early as 1880 they were known as St. Mark's Church and then Gorton Athletic in 1884.
Address: City of Manchester Stadium, Sport City, Manchester M11 3FF.
Ground capacity: 47,500.
Club Tel: 0870 062 1894.
Ticket Off: 0870 062 1894.

City Legends

1980s Paul Power
(1973-1986) Paul (above) turned out 445 times in midfield and was captain for six years. Player of the Year in 1981 and 1985.
1990s Georgi Kinkladze
(1995–1998) The midfielder is regarded by many as the greatest player in light blue,

but couldn't stop City being relegated twice before being sold to Ajax for £5.5m.
2000s Shaun Goater
(1998-2003) The Bermudan (below) scored more than 100 goals, including a play-off semi winner against Wigan in 1999.

Club Honours

Division One: 1937, 1968, 2002 (below).

Division Two: 1899, 1903, 1910, 1928, 1947, 1966.
FA Cup: 1904, 1934, 1956, 1969.
League Cup: 1970, 1976.
European Cup Winners' Cup: 1970.

Record transfers

In: £10m to Paris St. Germain for Nicolas Anelka, (right) June 2002.
Out: £7m from Fenerbahce for Nicolas Anelka, January 2005.

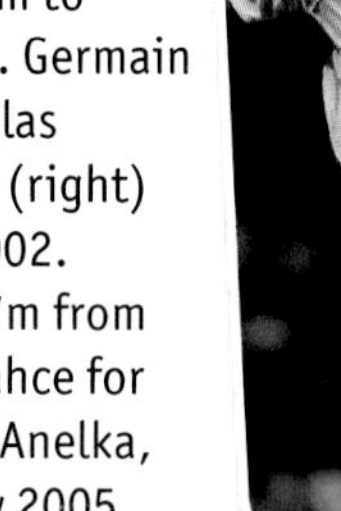

Young star

Midfielder Lee Croft (above) has been capped at England schoolboy level more times than any other player. He only made his Premiership debut in October 2005, but has since earned a long-term contract.

Did you know?

The Summerbee family have provided three generations of players to City: grandfather George, father Mike and son Nicky.

Season 2005-06

Premiership: 15th.
Top scorers: Darius Vassell and Andy Cole, both 10.
Player of the Year: Richard Dunne.

All you need to know about The... RED DEVILS

The History

Man United are one of the younger clubs as they were created in 1902. But most historians list their start date as 1878 when they were formed as Newton Heath Cricket and Football Club.
Address: Old Trafford, Sir Matt Busby Way, Manchester M16 0RA.
Ground capacity: 76,000.
Club Tel: 0161 868 8000.
Ticket Off: 0870 442 1994.

United Legends

1980s Bryan Robson
(1981-1994) Robbo (below) was Britain's most expensive player when he signed from West Brom for £1.75m. The midfield battler was nicknamed Captain Marvel and played 434 games before moving to Boro as player-manager.

1990s Roy Keane
(1993-2005) One of the finest midfielders of his time, the Republic of Ireland captain (below) won nine major honours during his time at Old Trafford. Inducted into the English Football Hall of Fame.

2000s Wayne Rooney
(2004-present) He could end up costing United £30m but, if he maintains his current development, it will be cash well spent. The former Everton youngster (left) has skill, strength, speed... the complete player.

Club Honours

Premiership: 1993, 1994, 1996, 1997, 1999, 2000, 2001, 2003.
Division One: 1908, 1911, 1952, 1956, 1957, 1965, 1967.
Division Two: 1936, 1975.
FA Cup: 1909, 1948, 1963, 1977, 1983, 1985, 1990, 1994, 1996, 1999, 2004.
League Cup: 1992, 2006.
European Cup: 1968.
Champions League: 1999 (below).

European Cup Winners' Cup: 1991.
Super Cup: 1991.
Inter-Continental Cup: 1999.

Record transfers

In: £30m to Leeds for Rio Ferdinand, July 2002.
Out: £25m from Real Madrid for David Beckham, July 2003.

Young star

American-born, but an Italian Under-19 striker, Giuseppe Rossi can also play in midfield or as a winger. Signed from Parma, he has pace and skill.

Did you know?

United's Holland keeper Edwin van der Sar was the first non-Italian to keep goal for Juventus.

Season 2005-06

Premiership: 2nd
Top scorer: Ruud Van Nistelrooy, 24 (below).
Player of the Year: Wayne Rooney.

BORN: November 29, 1973, Cardiff.
HEIGHT: 5ft 11in. **WEIGHT:** 11st.
PREVIOUS CLUBS: United since trainee.
DID YOU KNOW? Although Giggsy turned out for England Schoolboys, he later changed allegiance to Wales Youth, Under-21 and seniors, winning 56 caps.

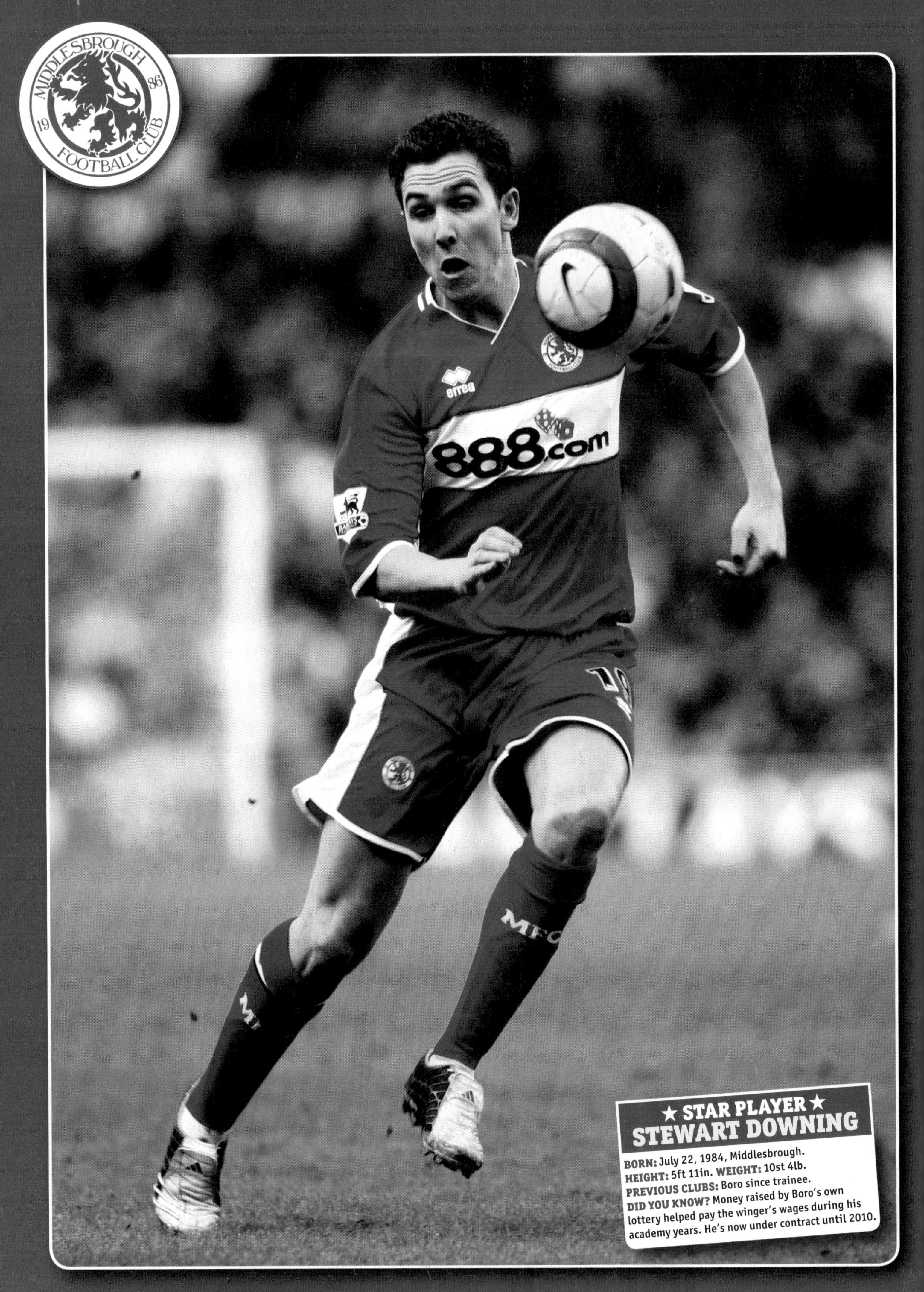

★ STAR PLAYER ★
STEWART DOWNING

BORN: July 22, 1984, Middlesbrough.
HEIGHT: 5ft 11in. **WEIGHT:** 10st 4lb.
PREVIOUS CLUBS: Boro since trainee.
DID YOU KNOW? Money raised by Boro's own lottery helped pay the winger's wages during his academy years. He's now under contract until 2010.

All you need to know about... THE BORO

The History
Members of Middlesbrough Cricket Club formed the football side in 1875. Current chairman Steve Gibson saved them from liquidation in 1986 and paid for their new ground.
Address: Riverside Stadium, Middlesbrough TS3 6RS.
Ground capacity: 35,120.
Club Tel: 0870 421 1986.
Ticket Off: 0870 421 1986.

Boro Legends

1980s Gary Pallister
(1984-1989, 1998-2001) Defender Gary (above) played over 200 games for his local club. Had nine successful years at Man United after a then-British record £2.3m transfer.
1990s Juninho
(1995-1997, 1999-2000, 2002-04) Boro loved the tiny

midfielder (above) so much they signed him three times. Brazilian Footballer of the Year 1994.
2000s Gareth Southgate
(2001-06) Steve McClaren's first signing, the former England man (below) has hung

up his boots and taken over from his boss. Replaced Paul Ince as captain in 2002 and became the first skipper to lift a major trophy for Boro, the Carling Cup in 2004. Infamous for his Euro 96 penalty miss.

Club Honours
Division One: 1995.

Division Two: 1927, 1929, 1974.
League Cup: 2004 (above).

Record transfers
In: £8.1m to Empoli for Massimo Maccarone (above), July 2002.
Out: £12m from Atletico Madrid for Juninho, July 1997.

Young star
Many promising youngsters are coming through the Boro academy, but we've gone for England Under-19 defender Matthew Bates, who could be Gareth Southgate's heir. Good reader of the game and excellent in the air.

Did you know?
Former Boro and Republic of Ireland striker Bernie Slaven has railings from their old Ayresome Park ground at the bottom of his garden.

Season 2005-06
Premiership: 14th.
Top scorer:
Ayegbeni Yakubu, 19 (below).
Player of the Year:
Ayegbeni Yakubu.

All you need to know about... THE MAGPIES

The History
The name Newcastle United appeared in 1892 when Newcastle East End and West End clubs combined. They were known as Stanley from 1881.
Address: St. James' Park, Newcastle-upon-Tyne NE1 4ST.
Ground capacity: 52,387.
Club Tel: 0191 201 8400.
Ticket Off: 0191 261 1571.

Newcastle Legends
1980s Kevin Keegan (1982–1984) Worshipped as a player and manager, Kevin (below) took the club to promotion in both roles and, as boss, saved them from a first appearance in the old Division Three.

1990s Peter Beardsley (1983–1987, 1993-1997) One of the finest creative

midfielders and goalscorers to pull on the famous black and white, Peter (above) now works with the youth team.
2000s Alan Shearer (1996–2006) What more can you say? Alan (below) scored 206 goals in ten years with

The Magpies to beat the club's previous best of 200 set by Jackie Milburn in the 1950s.

Club Honours
Division One: 1905, 1907, 1909, 1927, 1993.
Division Two: 1965.
FA Cup: 1910, 1924, 1932, 1951, 1952, 1955 (below).
European Fairs Cup: 1969.

Record transfers

In: £17m to Real Madrid for Michael Owen (left), August 2005.
Out: £13.6m from Real Madrid for Jonathan Woodgate, August 2004.

Young star
French teenager Charles N'Zogbia was snatched on a free from Le Havre, although the club later had to pay a compensation fee for the tricky midfielder who they have tied down on a long-term contract.

Did you know?
United stars Kieron Dyer, Alan Shearer and Patrick Kluivert appeared as themselves in the 2005 film *Goal*, partly filmed at St. James' Park.

Season 2005-06
Premiership: 7th.
Top goalscorer: Alan Shearer, 14.
Player of the Year: Shay Given (below).

★ STAR PLAYER ★
SCOTT PARKER

BORN: October 13, 1980, Lambeth.
HEIGHT: 5ft 9in. **WEIGHT:** 11st 10lb.
PREVIOUS CLUBS: Charlton Athletic, Norwich City (loan), Chelsea.
DID YOU KNOW? As a 13-year-old, Scott showed off his ball skills in a McDonalds advert during the 1994 World Cup finals.

★ STAR PLAYER ★
LOMANA LUA LUA

BORN: December 28, 1980, DR Congo.
HEIGHT: 5ft 8in. **WEIGHT:** 12st.
PREVIOUS CLUBS: Colchester United, Newcastle United.
DID YOU KNOW? Louie sought asylum in England at the age of eight as his dad's life was in danger in Zaire (now Congo).

All you need to know about... POMPEY

The History
In 1898, a local solicitor and five businessmen bought a plot of land for just under £5,000 and built Fratton Park. The next year they joined the Southern League.
Address: Fratton Park, Frogmore Road, Portsmouth, Hampshire PO4 8RA.
Ground capacity: 20,220.
Club Tel: 02392 731 204.
Ticket Off: 0871 230 1898.

Pompey Legends
1980s Vince Hilaire
(1984-1988) The former Crystal Palace winger (below) played 146 games for Pompey and hit 25 goals.

1990s Alan Knight
(1978-2000) His 801 games for Pompey is a record at a single club for a keeper. Won an MBE for his loyalty. Alan (above) is now coach at FC Dallas in the USA.

2000s Gary O'Neill
(1999-present) The writing appeared to be on the wall when England Under-21 star Gary (below) went on loan to Walsall and Cardiff. But he returned as a vital cog in midfield.

Club Honours
Division One: 1949, 1950, 2003 (below).

Division Three: 1962, 1983.
Division Three (S): 1924.
FA Cup: 1939.

Record transfers
In: £4.1m to Auxerre for Benjani Mwaruwari (left), January 2006.
Out: £7.5m from Middlesbrough for Ayegbeni Yakubu, August 2005.

Young star
Attacking midfielder Daryl Fordyce had a brief spell on loan at Bournemouth last term. But he's already made his mark for Northern Ireland Under-19s, having scored four against Serbia and Montenegro and two against Moldova.

Did you know?
Sir Arthur Conan Doyle (below), the Sherlock Holmes author, was one of Pompey's founders and even kept goal for them.

Season 2005-06
Premiership: 17th.
Top scorers: Gary O'Neill, Lomana Lua Lua (below) and Matt Taylor, all 7.
Player of the Year: Gary O'Neill.

All you need to know about... THE ROYALS

The History
Formed at a public meeting in 1871, the club later swallowed up local sides Reading Hornets and Earley FC.
Address: Madejski Stadium, Reading, RG2 0FL.
Ground capacity: 24,200.
Club Tel: 0118 968 1100.
Ticket office: 0870 999 1871.

Royals Legends
1980s Neil Webb
(1979-1982) Made his debut in February 1980 and became Reading's youngest League goalscorer six months later.

A fans' poll named Neil (above) in their best-ever XI. Later played for Pompey, Nottingham Forest and Manchester United.
1990s Phil Parkinson
(1992–2003) Voted by fans as one of the club's most popular

stars, Parky (above) was part of two promotion-winning sides before leaving for Colchester.
2000s Graeme Murty
(1998-present) Skipper (below) as the side reached the Premiership for the first

time. His second goal for the club in 280 games, a last day penalty, ensured a record 106 points tally.

Club Honours
Championship: 2006 (above).
Division Two: 1994.
Division Three: 1986.
Division Three (S): 1926.
Division Four: 1979.

Record transfers
In: £1m to Bristol City for Leroy Lita, July 2005.
Out: £1.5m from Newcastle for Shaka Hislop (above), August 1995.

Young star
Signed for around £80,000 from Cork City, Kevin Doyle proved to be one of the bargains of 2005-06, scoring 18 goals for The Royals.

Did you know?
The metal posts topped with cylindrical discs surrounding The Madejski are vents to release underground build-up of methane gases, as the stadium was built on a waste dump.

Season 2005-06

Championship: Champions.
Top scorer:
Dave Kitson, 22.
Player of the Year:
Kevin Doyle (below).

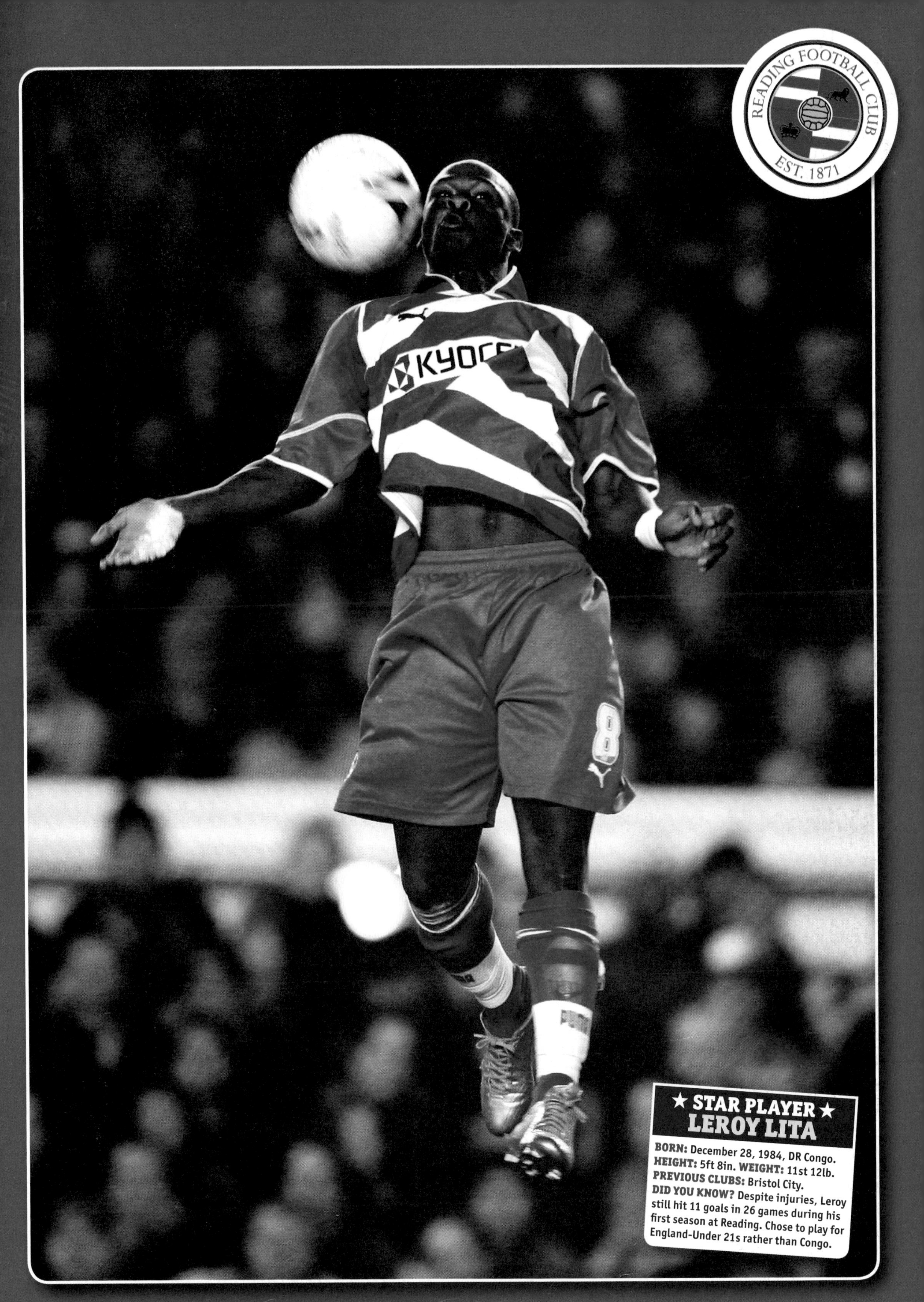

★ STAR PLAYER ★
LEROY LITA

BORN: December 28, 1984, DR Congo.
HEIGHT: 5ft 8in. **WEIGHT:** 11st 12lb.
PREVIOUS CLUBS: Bristol City.
DID YOU KNOW? Despite injuries, Leroy still hit 11 goals in 26 games during his first season at Reading. Chose to play for England-Under 21s rather than Congo.

BORN: December 28, 1981, Manchester.
HEIGHT: 5ft 9in. **WEIGHT:** 10st 3lb.
PREVIOUS CLUBS: Manchester United, Port Vale (loan), Watford.
DID YOU KNOW? Danny played three times for Man United before his move to Watford, who sold him for £500,000.

All you need to know about... THE BLADES

The History

Charles Stokes, a member of Yorkshire County Cricket Club, formed Sheffield United in 1889 after watching an FA Cup semi-final between Preston North End and West Brom.

Address: Bramall Lane, Sheffield, S2 4SU.
Ground capacity: 33,000.
Club Tel: 0870 787 1960.
Ticket Off: 0870 787 1799.

Blades Legends

1980s Colin Morris

(1982-1988) The father of Lee Morris, The Blades' record transfer out, Colin (above) was an attacking midfielder noted for his pin-point crosses. Scored and missed more penalties than any other player.

1990s Alan Kelly

(1992-1999) Moved to United

from Preston for £150,000 and stayed despite Premiership relegation. Republic of Ireland keeper (above) played under five bosses at Bramall Lane.

2000s Phil Jagielka

(1999-present) Phil (below) was Blades'

fans Player of the Year for the past two seasons and 2005-06 Championship Player of the Season. Defender, midfielder and has even played as an emergency keeper.

Club Honours

Division One: 1898.
Division Two: 1953.
Division Four: 1982.
FA Cup: 1899, 1902, 1915, 1925 (below).

Record transfers

In: £2.5m (rising to possible £3m) to Preston for Claude Davis, June 2006.
Out: £3m from Derby for Lee Morris (left), October 1999.

Young star

Local lad Jonathan Forte (above right) has been out on loan twice to Doncaster and also had a spell with Rotherham. The 6ft tall, 20-year-old hitman has hit eight goals in 17 starts during his travels.

Did you know?

They get their nickname "The Blades" because of Sheffield's history of making stainless steel knives. The team emblem was designed by former boss Jimmy Sirrel and first used for the 1977-78 season.

Season 2005-06

Championship: Runners-up.

Top scorers: Neil Shipperley (above) and Danny Webber, (both 11).
Player of the Year: Phil Jagielka.

All you need to know about... SPURS

The History
Old boys of St. John's Presbyterian School and Tottenham Grammar formed Hotspur FC from a local cricket club in 1882.
Address: White Hart Lane, Bill Nicholson Way, 748 High Road, Tottenham, N17 0AP.
Ground capacity: 36,237.
Club Tel: 0870 420 5000.
Ticket Off: 0870 420 5000.

Spurs Legends
1980s Glenn Hoddle
(1974-1988) Glenn (below) joined as a schoolboy, scored on his debut and then became a cult hero at White Hart Lane. Later managed the club.

1990s Jurgen Klinsmann
(1994-1995, 1998) The German striker (above right), famed for his diving, enjoyed a golden 1995. He was England's Footballer of the Year, European Footballer of the Year runner-up and third in the World Player awards.
2000s Ledley King
(1997-present) Captain and the club's longest-serving player (below) having joined as a trainee at the age of 16. Ledley, contracted until 2010, excels in central defence or as a holding midfielder.

Club Honours
Division One: 1951, 1961.
Division Two: 1920, 1950.
FA Cup: 1901, 1921, 1961, 1962, 1967, 1981, 1982, 1991 (above).

League Cup: 1971, 1973, 1999.
UEFA Cup: 1972, 1984.
Cup Winners' Cup: 1963.

Record transfers
In: £11m to Dynamo Kiev for Sergei Rebrov, (left), May 2000.
Out: £5.5m from Lazio for Paul Gascoigne, May 1992.

Young star

Lee Barnard (above) had a taste of Premiership football last term after a few loan spells. The striker hit 17 goals in 17 starts for the reserves in 2004-05, including two hat-tricks.

Did you know?
Erik Thorstvedt became the Premiership's first-ever substitute when he replaced Ian Walker in goal on the opening day of 1992-93.

Season 2005-06
Premiership: 5th.
Top scorer: Robbie Keane, 16.
Player of the Year: Robbie Keane.

★ STAR PLAYER ★
PAUL ROBINSON

BORN: October 15, 1979, Beverley, Yorks.
HEIGHT: 6ft 4in. **WEIGHT:** 15st 7lb.
PREVIOUS CLUBS: Leeds United.
DID YOU KNOW? At Leeds, Robbo scored against Swindon in the 2003 League Cup to take the game to extra-time. His save in the penalty shoot-out won the tie.

★ STAR PLAYER ★
MATTHEW SPRING

BORN: November 17, 1979, Harlow, Essex.
HEIGHT: 5ft 11in. **WEIGHT:** 11st 7lb.
PREVIOUS CLUBS: Luton, Leeds United.
DID YOU KNOW? Watford boss Adrian Boothroyd bought Matthew from Leeds for £150,000 in 2005. They had worked as player and coach at Elland Road.

All you need to know about... THE HORNETS

The History

Began life as Watford Rovers in 1881, changed to West Herts in 1893, then took over Watford St. Mary's before taking current name in 1898.
Address: Vicarage Road, Watford WD18 0ER.
Ground capacity: 20,000.
Club Tel: 0870 111 1881.
Ticket Off: 0870 111 1881.

Watford Legends

1980s John Barnes
(1981-1987) Arguably the best player to turn out for the club, the winger (below) left Watford for Liverpool and established himself as an England regular.

1990s Gary Porter
(1983-1996) During his 13 years' service, the midfielder

(above) made an amazing 464 appearances. Once scored a second half hat-trick against Bolton when the club were 0-3 down, and they won 4-3

2000s Marlon King
(2005–present) Marlon (below) is the first Watford player since

Luther Blissett in the 1980s to score more than 20 League goals in a season. His strikes ensured their place in the play-offs last season.

Club Honours

Division Two: 1998 (above).
Division Three: 1969.
Division Four: 1978.

Record transfers

In: £2.25m to Spurs in August 2000 for Alan Nielsen.
Out: £2.3m from Chelsea for Paul Furlong (left), May 1994.

Young star

Youth academy product Ashley Young can play

wide or as an out-and-out striker. Ashley (above) was named the club's Player of the Year for season 2004–05, last term he hit 14 goals in 41 starts to attract the big club scouts.

Did you know?

Boss Graham Taylor took the club from Division Four to the old Division One and the FA Cup Final during his first spell in charge. When he returned, he lifted them from Division Two to the Premiership in two seasons.

Season 2005-06

Championship: 3rd (Play-off winners, 3-0 v Leeds United).
Top scorer:
Marlon King, 21.
Player of the Year:
Marlon King.

All you need to know about... THE HAMMERS

The History
Formed by shipbuilders as Thames Ironworks FC in 1895 but decided to turn professional five years later and became West Ham United.
Address: The Boleyn Ground, Green Street, Upton Park, London E13 9AZ.
Ground capacity: 34,500.
Club Tel: 0208 548 2748.
Ticket Off: 0870 112 2700.

Hammers Legends
1980s Tony Cottee
(1984-1988, 1994-1996)
PFA Young Player of the Year in 1986, Tony (below) joined Everton for a British record £2.2m in 1988 after 118 goals in 256 games.

1990s Julian Dicks
(1988-1993, 1994-1996) Four times West Ham Player of the Year, the hardman defender (above) spent one forgettable season at Liverpool. Forced to retire through injury, his knee problem prevented him becoming a golf professional.
2000s Marlon Harewood
(2003-present) The fans just love the hard-working striker (below left) signed from Forest for just £500,000. His goals were vital to them reaching, and then staying, in the Premiership last term.

Club Honours
Division Two: 1958, 1981.

FA Cup: 1964, 1975, 1980 (above).
Cup Winners' Cup: 1965.

Record transfers
In: £7.25m to Norwich City for Dean Ashton, January 2006.
Out: £18m from Leeds United for Rio Ferdinand, (right) November 2000.

Young star

Hogan Ephraim (above), an attacking midfielder, has come through the Upton Park academy. A hit at England Under-17 level with nine goals in 19 games, he is now with the Under-18s.

Did you know?
Defender Alvin Martin scored a hat-trick against three different Newcastle keepers in 1986. Martin Thomas was injured, his replacement Peter Beardsley also had to go off and finally Chris Hedworth took over as The Hammers won 8-1.

Season 2005-06
Premiership: 9th.
Top scorer:
Marlon Harewood, 16.
Player of the Year:
Danny Gabbidon.

★ STAR PLAYER ★
DEAN ASHTON

BORN: November 24, 1983, Swindon.
HEIGHT: 6ft 2in. **WEIGHT:** 12st 8lb.
PREVIOUS CLUBS: Crewe, Norwich.
DID YOU KNOW? Deano left Crewe for £3m in 2005 after coming through their famous youth system. They got a further £1.5m when he moved to West Ham.

WIGAN ATHLETIC

★ STAR PLAYER ★
ARJAN DE ZEEUW

BORN: April 16, 1970, Holland.
HEIGHT: 6ft. **WEIGHT:** 13st 6lb.
PREVIOUS CLUBS: Telstar, Barnsley, Portsmouth.
DID YOU KNOW? Arjan is in his second spell with Wigan having played for them from 1999 to 2001 before Pompey called.

All you need to know about... THE LATICS

The History
Wigan Borough resigned from the League in 1931 and the following year was reborn as Wigan Athletic. Elected to the Football League in 1978.
Address: JJB Stadium, Wigan WN5 0UZ.
Ground capacity: 25,000.
Club Tel: 01942 774 000.
Ticket Off: 0870 112 2552.

Wigan Legends
1980s Paul Jewell
(1984-1988) The current boss (below) cost £15,000 from

Liverpool and hit 35 goals in 137 games. Went to Bradford City for £80,000.
1990s David Lowe
(1982-1987, 1996-1999) David (above right) won the Freight Rover Trophy with an overhead kick during his first spell at the

club. Became their record League goalscorer in 1998 with 66 and won the Division Three title. Later became a coach at the JJB.
2000s Leighton Baines
England Under-21 defender (below) joined the club at

the age of 16 and has just agreed a new deal to 2009. Has played in every division from Two to the Premiership.

Club Honours
Division Two: 2003 (below).

Division Three: 1997.
Freight Rover Trophy: 1985.
Auto Windscreens Shield: 1999.

Record transfers
In: £5.5m to Birmingham for Emile Heskey, July 2006.
Out: £3m from Man United for Roy Carroll (right), July 2001.

Young star
Defender Kevin Lee signed as a trainee in 2004 and has already been loaned out to Accrington Stanley and Blackpool for experience.

Did you know?
Wigan's first appearance in a major final was at the 2006 Carling Cup when they were thrashed 4-0 by neighbours Manchester United at Cardiff's Millennium Stadium.

Season 2005-06
Premiership: 10th.
Top scorer:
Jason Roberts, 14 (below).
Player of the Year:
Arjan De Zeeuw.

THE HIGHS AND LOWS

Every Football club has seasons to remember, thanks to promotion, spectacular cup runs or even a league title. Managers become heroes, players legends and supporters danced in the streets. We chart days you want to remember and forget!

BARNSLEY

HIGH: 1997
Runners-up in Division One for promotion to the Premiership under Danny Wilson. The skills of Clint Marcelle and Neil Redfearn (left) spawned the terrace chant of "Just like watching Brazil" at Oakwell. Just beats last season's play-off victory against Swansea.

LOW: 2002
The Tykes dropped back into the third tier of English football for the first time in more than 20 years.

BIRMINGHAM CITY

HIGH: 2002
Gained promotion to the Premiership (below) and achieved survival with the help of French World Cup-winner Christophe Dugarry. In 1963, City won the League Cup, defeating arch-rivals Aston Villa over two legs.

LOW: 1989
Birmingham were relegated to Division Three for the first time in their history after years of yo-yoing between the top two leagues.

BURNLEY

HIGH: 1960
The Clarets became Champions (below) for only the second time in their history under the stewardship of legendary manager Harry Potts.

LOW: 1984
Burnley found themselves in English football's basement division for the first time after relegation from the then Third Division.

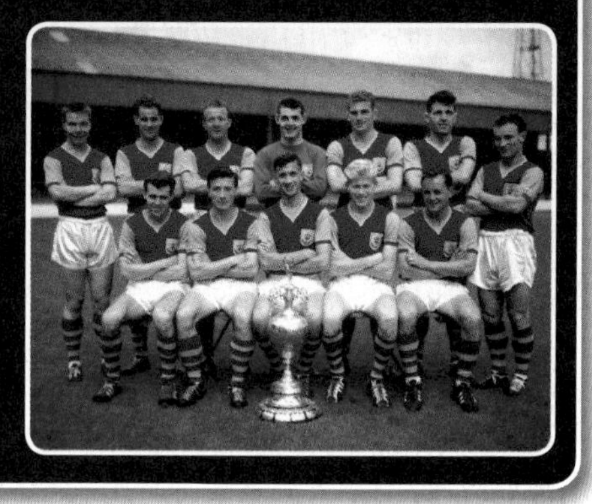

CARDIFF CITY

HIGH: 2003
Promotion to The Championship after a thrilling play-off victory over QPR at the Millennium Stadium (below). Also FA Cup-winners in 1927, after beating Arsenal 1-0.

LOW: 1986
Dropped into the old Fourth Division after years of struggle on the pitch and financially. Crowds at Ninian Park averaged 3,000.

COLCHESTER UNITED

HIGH: 2006
Boss Phil Parkinson (below) led the U's to runner-up spot in League Two and earned them a place in league football's second tier for the first-time ever. Also gave Champions Chelsea a scare in the FA Cup.

LOW: 1990
The U's slipped out of the Football League after a poor season meant relegation to the Conference.

COVENTRY CITY

HIGH: 1987
John Sillett guided the club to FA Cup success after a 3-2 victory over Spurs. Keith Houchen (below) scored a spectacular diving header, but an own-goal by Gary Mabbutt secured the trophy for the Sky Blues.

LOW: 2001
Relegation from the Premiership under Gordon Strachan after 34 years in the top-flight. The departures of Gary McAllister, to Liverpool, Robbie Keane to Inter Milan and Mustapha Hadji to Villa.

CRYSTAL PALACE

HIGH: 1990
Palace reached the FA Cup Final and forced Man United to a replay, having already beaten the best side in the country at that time, Liverpool, 4-3, in a memorable semi-final. The London club also finished a respectable 15th in the First Division that season, in spite of a disastrous start to the campaign which included a thumping 9-0 defeat to the reigning league champions Liverpool at Anfield.

LOW: 1998
Relegation when a temporary and inexperienced managerial team of former Sweden World Cup Star Tomas Brolin and Italian winger Atillio Lombardo (pictured) took charge of the club at the tail end of the season.

DERBY COUNTY

HIGH: 1971
Hearing they had won the league under Brian Clough – whilst away on their holidays! The Rams had finished their season early but Liverpool and Leeds both failed to gain the points they needed to take the First Division title. Derby repeated the feat in 1975 under Dave Mackay.

LOW: 1991
After four years in the First Division, Derby were relegated (below) and forced to sell stars like Dean Saunders and Mark Wright to balance the books.

HULL CITY

HIGH: 2005
Gaining promotion to The Championship under Peter Taylor. Local hero Nicky Barmby (left) returned to his home-town club as they secured back-to-back promotions.

LOW: 1996
The club were relegated to the basement division for the second time in their history and only managed to score 36 goals and earn a paltry 31 points.

IPSWICH TOWN

HIGH: 1981
Town claimed the UEFA Cup (right) under the stewardship of Bobby Robson and inspired by the goal-scoring exploits of John Wark. Also, Sir Alf Ramsey took them to the First Division title in 1962, before becoming England boss.

LOW: 1995
Relegation from the Premier League under George Burley, which included an embarrassing Premiership record 9-0 defeat to Manchester United at Old Trafford.

LEEDS UNITED

HIGH: 1974
Winning the League under Don Revie, after three consecutive seasons as runners-up. Legends such as Jack Charlton, Peter Lorimer and Billy Bremner provided the spine of the side.

LOW: 2003
The agony of relegation from the Premiership. Just two seasons earlier an exciting young side, guided by manager David O'Leary, had reached the semi-finals of the Champions League. They spent millions to challenge for the title, but faced financial ruin after failing to reach the tournament in 2002.

LEICESTER CITY

HIGH: 1997
Their second League Cup victory, when Martin O'Neill's side defeated Middlesbrough at Hillsborough after a replay. They won 1-0 thanks to an extra-time strike from Steve Claridge (below).

LOW: 2001
Top of the Premiership in October, they suffered an FA Cup quarter-final home defeat to Second Division Wycombe (above). Boss Peter Taylor was replaced by Micky Adams and Dave Bassett, but The Foxes slumped to relegation.

LUTON TOWN

HIGH: 1998
A Brian Stein-inspired side defeated the might of Arsenal in the League Cup Final at Wembley (below). Two goals from Stein and another from Danny Wilson helped The Hatters claim their first major honour.

LOW: 1965
Town slumped into football's basement division, only six years after making an FA Cup Final appearance.

NORWICH CITY

HIGH: 1993
Mike Walker took The Canaries to third in the debut Premier League. In the following year's UEFA Cup, they had an amazing 2-1 away win at German giants Bayern Munich, thanks to a wonder goal from midfielder Jeremy Goss (pictured with Walker below).

LOW: 1994
Relegated to Division One having dropped from seventh place at Christmas. Their second half of the season slump, included a run of seven successive defeats under John Deehan.

PLYMOUTH ARGYLE

HIGH: 2004
The Pilgrims were champions of Division Two (below) with an impressive 90 points. Paul Sturrock had been in charge for most of the season before leaving for Southampton and the title was secured in the last game under Bobby Williamson. Also, in 1984, reached the FA Cup semi-final as a Third Division club.

LOW: 1998
Plymouth's worst campaign ended with relegation to the Football League's lowest division.

PRESTON NORTH END

HIGH: 1889
Claimed the League and FA Cup double way back in 1889 (above). In 2000 David Moyes guided North End to the second tier of English football after many years in the bottom two divisions.

LOW: 1986
North End finished 91st out of the 92 Football League clubs, but avoided relegation to the Conference after they were re-elected.

QUEENS PARK RANGERS

HIGH: 1993
The highest-placed London club in the Premiership (fifth). Won the League Cup in 1967 as a Third Division club, legend Rodney Marsh scoring in the final, as they defeated West Brom 3-2. Also gained promotion that season as champions.

LOW: 2001
The Hoops dropped down into what is now League One (left), and also entered financial administration, making it a year to forget.

SHEFFIELD WEDNESDAY

HIGH: 1991
The Owls won the League Cup and gained promotion to the First Division under Ron Atkinson. Wednesday beat Man United in the final (below) with a team containing David Hirst, Carlton Palmer, Nigel Pearson, Peter Shirtliff and Chris Turner. The winning goal came from midfielder John Sheridan.

LOW: 2002
They crashed into League One, just three years after gracing the Premiership. It was only the second time they had sunk to the third tier. Ironically, their manager was Chris Turner, the keeper who starred in the 1991 League Cup win.

SOUTHAMPTON

HIGH: 1976
Winning the FA Cup, when they beat Manchester United 1-0 thanks to a Bobby Stokes goal. Saints had finished sixth in Division Two and United were third in the First Division at the time.

LOW: 2005
Relegation under Harry Redknapp, who had jumped ship from local rivals Portsmouth in a vain attempt to save them from the drop. The Saints were demoted (right) after more than 20 years of top-flight football.

SOUTHEND UNITED

HIGH: 2006
The Shrimpers finished champions of League One and gained promotion to The Championship. It is their first time at that level since 1997, thanks to manager Steve Tilson, and the goal-scoring feats of Freddie Eastwood (left).

LOW: 1998
Under former Hammer Alvin Martin, the Essex side dropped down into the bottom division, which sealed successive relegations.

STOKE CITY

HIGH: 1972
League Cup success (right) after defeating favourites Chelsea 2-1 under the guidance of manager Tony Waddington. They played 11 games on their way to the final, including a twice replayed two-legged semi against West Ham, which included a memorable penalty save by Gordon Banks from his fellow World Cup-winner Geoff Hurst.

LOW: 1991
FIFTEENTH in the then Division Three, the club's lowest-ever finish. Former England midfielder Alan Ball departed as manager half-way through a disappointing season which had followed relegation.

SUNDERLAND

HIGH: 1973
FA Cup Final victory over Leeds thanks to the only goal of the game by Ian Porterfield. Bob Stokoe's side were a league below their opponents and keeper Jimmy Montgomery is remembered for a stunning double save.

LOW: 2006
Relegation from the Premiership (right), beating their own record for the worst-ever points total with a miserly 15. The Black Cats were effectively down at Christmas and it got worse when bitter local rivals Newcastle beat them twice.

WEST BROM

HIGH: 1968
Baggies legend Jeff Astle (below left) scored the only goal in the FA Cup Final against Everton and they also finished eighth in the league.

LOW: 1991
Relegated to Division Three under Brian Talbot with a meagre 48 points from 46 games.

WOLVES

HIGH: 1954
Wolves were labelled Champions of the world by the *Daily Mail* following their 3-2 victory over Hungarian champions Honved (above) under manager Stan Cullis. The win came before the introduction of formal European competitions. Also, League champions three times in the 1950s.

LOW: 1986
The Molineux club were consigned to the basement division after their third successive relegation.

A LEAGUE OF THEIR OWN

Every dog has its day, or so they say. And the same applies to teams currently in the Football League's third tier. We chart the champagne moments that, even today, fans still regard as the defining periods of their club's history...

BLACKPOOL 1953
The FA Cup victory in the "Matthews Final", named after the legendary Blackpool and Stoke winger Sir Stanley Matthews. Stan Mortensen grabbed a hat-trick as The Tangerines beat Bolton 4-3, from 3-1 down.

BOURNEMOUTH 1987
Promotion to the then-Division Two, under Harry Redknapp, who developed his wheeler-dealer skills at Dean Court. The Cherries also defeated big hitters Man United in a third round home FA Cup tie in 1986.

BRADFORD CITY 2000
Premiership survival on the last day of the season having been favourites for relegation. It was the Bantams' first season in the big league thanks to Paul Jewell.

BRENTFORD 1992
The Bees claimed the Third Division championship and promotion to the new First Division, with striker Dean Holdsworth playing a major part. Also, reached the FA Cup quarter-finals in 1989.

BRIGHTON 1979
Secured promotion to the top-flight and stayed there for three seasons. In 1983, they reached the FA Cup Final for the first time and took Man United to a replay.

BRISTOL CITY 1998
The Robins gained promotion to Division One under John Ward and Terry Connor. They prepared for the First Division by making the club's first £1m signing, Ade Akinbiyi for £1.2m from Gillingham.

CARLISLE UNITED 1974
Promotion to the top-flight after finishing third in the old Second Division under manager Alan Ashman. They stayed there just one season.

CHELTENHAM 2006
Play-off victory promotion to League One under John Ward. But in 2002, Steve Cotterill took them to the same division after another play-off final win and a record FA Cup run to the fifth round.

CHESTERFIELD 1998
Reached the FA Cup semi-finals as a Second Division club under John Duncan only to lose to Boro in a replay. In the first game at Old Trafford Chesterfield had a goal ruled out by referee David Elleray who said it hadn't crossed the line. TV replays showed it had.

CREWE ALEXANDRA 1998
Under long-serving manager Dario Gradi, in charge since 1983, they finished 11th in the First Division, now known as The Championship. It was their highest-ever finish aided by players like Dele Adebola.

DONCASTER 2004

Division Two Champions under Dave Penney. It sealed successive promotions, after they had come up though the Conference play-offs the season before. Rovers racked up an impressive 92 points.

GILLINGHAM 2000

The Gills reached the First Division for the first time in their history after success in the play-offs where they beat Wigan 3-2 after extra-time, thanks to goals from Steve Butler and Andy Thomson.

HUDDERSFIELD 1922

The Terriers claimed their only FA Cup victory. But during the 1920s Herbert Chapman became the only manager to win three successive First Division titles with the same club, until Sir Alex Ferguson achieved the feat in 2001 with Man United.

LEYTON ORIENT 1962

The O's reached the First Division after finishing runners-up to Liverpool.

MILLWALL 2004

A young side guided by player-manager Dennis Wise (far left) reached the FA Cup Final, where they bravely lost 3-0 to Man United. Also, winning the Second Division title under John Docherty in 1998, largely thanks to the goals of Teddy Sheringham and Tony Cascarino.

NORTHAMPTON TOWN 1965

Gained promotion to the First Division as Second Division runners-up, as David Bowen took them to the highest level in their history.

NOTTINGHAM FOREST 1980

Forest became the second English club to retain the European Cup. They won against Malmo in 1979 thanks to a Trevor Francis header, and a John Robertson goal gave them victory against Hamburg the following season. Also League and League Cup winners in 1978, all results under the legendary Brian Clough.

OLDHAM 1990

Under Joe Royle, The Latics enjoyed a great spell in the early 1990s. with players such as Andy Ritchie (right) Ian Marshall, Roger Palmer and Rick Holden. The highlights were two FA Cup semi-final defeats to Man United and reaching the League Cup Final in 1990 as a Second Division side, where they were beaten 1-0 by Nottingham Forest.

PORT VALE 1998

Vale knocked First Division Spurs out of the FA Cup in the fourth round and the following season were promoted to the Second Division after a third place finish and a play-off victory.

ROTHERHAM 2001

Runners-up in Division Two and gained promotion to the First Division under Ronnie Moore.

SCUNTHORPE 1962

The highest league finish for The Irons was when they claimed fourth in the old Second Division under Dick Duckworth.

SWANSEA CITY 1982

An impressive sixth in the top-flight under John Toshack, who had secured promotion for the Welsh club the previous season.

TRANMERE 2000

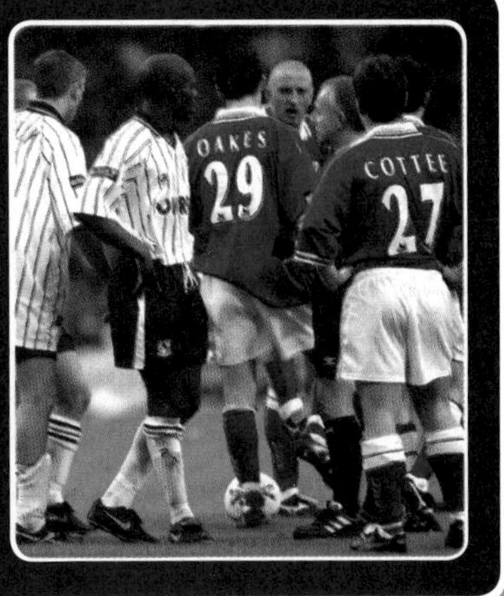

Rovers reached the League Cup Final, where John Aldridge's side lost 2-1 to Leicester City, but gave an excellent account of themselves. Their best league finish was fourth spot in Division One in 1993.

YEOVIL TOWN 2005

The Huish Park club gained promotion to League One in 2005 under Gary Johnson, having secured the League Two title only two seasons after promotion to the League from the Conference.

MAGICAL MOMENTS

And now we come to the basement clubs (sorry lads!) But from Accrington Stanley right through to Wycombe Wanderers there are still more than a few tales of success sitting in their history books...

ACCRINGTON STANLEY 2006
Accrington Stanley won the Conference, 11 points clear at the top, to return to the Football League after a gap of 44 years.

BARNET 1991
Promotion to the League for the first time under boss Barry Fry. They secured the Conference Championship after being runners-up on three occasions.

BOSTON UNITED 2002
Steve Evans took them up to the League, despite an investigation into alleged financial irregularities.

BRISTOL ROVERS 1995
With John Ward in charge, Rovers managed their highest-ever league finish, claiming fourth place in the Second Division.

BURY 1925
The Shakers finished fourth in the top-flight over 80 years ago. Back in 1900 and 1903 they won the FA Cup.

CHESTER CITY 1994
Runners-up in Division Three and promoted under boss Graham Barrow.

DARLINGTON 1990
The Quakers fans returned to the Football League as Conference Champions under former Leicester City and Aston Villa boss Brian Little.

GRIMSBY 1998
Auto Windscreen Shield victory over Bournemouth at Wembley (below) They also finished in fifth place in the top-flight in 1935.

HARTLEPOOL 2003
Mike Newell took Pools to the Second Division as runners-up in the Third.

HEREFORD UNITED 1972
Their famous Third Round FA Cup replay victory over Newcastle thanks to a Ronnie Radford strike.

LINCOLN CITY 1998
Promotion to Division Two with John Beck in charge and Gareth Ainsworth starring on the pitch.

MACCLESFIELD TOWN 1998
The Silkmen were runners-up in Division Three and gained promotion to the Second Division under former Man United and Northern Ireland star Sammy McIlroy.

MANSFIELD TOWN 1977
The Stags secured the Third Division championship under Peter Morris.

MK DONS 1988
As Wimbledon (left) winning the FA Cup by beating Liverpool 1-0 thanks to a Lawrie Sanchez header. They also finished seventh in the top-flight.

NOTTS COUNTY 1991
Promoted to the First Division after winning the play-offs under Neil Warnock, thanks to the goal scoring efforts of Tommy Johnson and Tony Agana. The Magpies won the FA Cup back in 1894.

PETERBOROUGH 1993
Posh finished tenth in the First Division, now The Championship, having gained promotion from Division Two the previous season.

ROCHDALE 1962
Dale reached the League Cup Final at Wembley as a Fourth Division club but Second Division Norwich City beat them 4-0 after a two-legged final.

SHREWSBURY TOWN 1984
The Gay Meadow club claimed eighth spot in the Second Division in both 1984 and 1985, their highest-ever finish.

STOCKPORT COUNTY 1998
David Jones took them to their highest-ever league finish, eighth in Division One, now The Championship.

SWINDON TOWN 1993
Arrival in the Premiership under Glenn Hoddle (below) after a play-off victory over Leicester. In 1969, The Robins beat Arsenal in the League Cup Final thanks to goals from Roger Smart and Don Rogers.

TORQUAY UNITED 2004
The Gulls flew into third place in League Two and promotion under manager Leroy Rosenior.

WALSALL 1999
Second in Division Two and promoted under manager Ray Graydon.

WREXHAM 1992
The Red Dragons slayed Champions Arsenal 2-1 in the FA Cup thanks to goals from Mickey Thomas (right) and Steve Watkin.

WYCOMBE WANDERERS 2001
Lawrie Sanchez was in charge as Wanderers reached the FA Cup semis, knocking out Leicester City on the way. Striker Roy Essandoh was famously recruited through Teletext, and scored the winning goal.

SHOOT ANNUAL 2007 – QUIZ ANSWERS

PAGE 20/21
TRIVIAL TEASERS
1. Paris
2. Leeds United
3. Paraguay
4. Crystal Palace
5. Alan Pardew
6. Yellow & green
7. Teddy Sheringham
8. Referees
9. Djibril Cisse
10. Sheffield United

HIDDEN FACES
A. Sam Allardyce
B. Steven Gerrard
C. Robin Van Persie
D. Mark Schwarzer
E. Paul Jewell
F. Owen Hargreaves

GOALMOUTH SCRAMBLE
1. AC Milan
2. Porto
3. Juventus
4. Marseille
5. Barcelona
6. Manchester United
7. Real Madrid
8. Bayern Munich
9. Borussia Dortmund
10. Liverpool

SPOT THE BALL (A2)

SPORTING VENUES
A. Fulham
B. Manchester United
C. Fulham
D. Sheffield United
E. Newcastle United

WHO SCORED?
David Beckham

NAME THAT YEAR
2003

MISSING LINKS
1. Leeds United
2. Robbie Fowler
3. Leicester City
4. David James
5. West Ham

PAGE 56/57
TRIVIAL TEASERS
1. Trinidad & Tobago
2. Gareth Southgate
3. Watford
4. Newcastle & Blackburn
5. Hull City
6. Steven Gerrard
7. Tottenham & West Ham
8. Spain
9. Wigan Athletic
10. Gary Neville

CELEBRITY FANS
A. Newcastle
B. West Ham
C. Aston Villa

TRUE OR FALSE
1. False
2. False
3. True

CROSSWORD
ACROSS 1. Niall. 4. Butt. 6. Carr. 10. Shola. 11. Foyle. 12. York. 13. Peter. 14. Fife. 17. Reading. 18. Scolari. 19. Vassell. 22. Gunners. 24. Ruud. 25. Drury. 26. Reid. 30. Emlyn. 31. Adams. 32. East. 33. Todd. 34. Kenny.

DOWN 1. Nicky. 2. Austria. 3. Lyon. 4. Boateng. 5. Toffees. 7. America. 8. Red Devils. 9. Ayr. 15. Pires. 16. Young. 17. Riverside. 20. Souness. 21. Lorenzo. 22. Gerrard. 23. Emerson.